The Way of The Sage: Awakening The Tao Within
Ancient Wisdom of Lao Tzu for the Modern World
Azariah Samuel A

The Way of The Sage: Awakening The Tao Within
Ancient Wisdom of Lao Tzu for the Modern World

The Way of The Sage

Azariah Samuel A

Published by Azariah Samuel A, 2024.

THE WAY OF THE SAGE

First edition. October 17, 2024.

Copyright © 2024 Azariah Samuel A.

ISBN: 979-8224157174

Written by Azariah Samuel A.

Table of Contents

Dedication

To Dad,
To all seekers of wisdom,
May you find the Tao within.

On Lao Tzu
The Way of the Sage: Awakening the Tao Within
Birds soar on feathered hope,
Their wings a gift from sky to earth.
Fish glide through liquid dreams,
Fins like silk in water's embrace.
Wild beasts run free and bold,
Feet drumming nature's heartbeat.
But life's path is not without thorns:
Traps lie in wait for running feet,
Nets yearn to catch the swimming free,
Arrows seek to ground the flying.
Yet dragons – ah, those mystic souls!
How do they climb heaven's ladder,
Dancing through clouds like smoke?
Their secret remains unwhispered.
Today, my eyes beheld a wonder:
The Sage, wise beyond mortal years.
In his presence, I saw clearly:
He is no man, but dragon-sage,
Bridging earth and sky with ease.
His wisdom flows like mountain streams,
His thoughts soar higher than eagles.
The Sage moves as mist through trees,
Untouchable, yet touching all.
In him, the Tao breathes and speaks,
A living map to inner peace.
He shows us how to spread our wings,
To swim in depths of our own hearts,
To run towards our truest selves.
The Sage, the dragon in man's form,
Invites us all to look within,
To find the dragon in our souls,
And rise above life's fleeting cares.

About the Author

Azariah Samuel A is a dedicated student of Taoist philosophy.

Introduction

Dear Reader,

Welcome to "The Way of the Sage: Awakening the Tao Within." This book is an invitation to explore the timeless wisdom of the Tao Te Ching, reimagined for our modern world. As you embark on this journey, you'll discover 81 original poems inspired by Lao Tzu's classic text, each accompanied by insights, practical applications, and reflections to deepen your understanding.

The Tao Te Ching, written over 2,500 years ago, continues to offer profound guidance for living in harmony with ourselves, others, and the natural world. Its teachings on simplicity, humility, and the art of effortless action (wu wei) are perhaps more relevant today than ever before.

In creating this book, I've sought to honor the spirit of the original text while making its wisdom accessible to contemporary readers. Each chapter offers a fresh perspective on a key Taoist concept, inviting you to contemplate its meaning and apply it to your daily life.

How to Use This Book

1. Read slowly and mindfully. Allow each poem and explanation to resonate within you.

2. Reflect on the questions provided at the end of each chapter. Consider journaling your thoughts.

3. Experiment with applying the principles in your daily life. Notice how your perspective shifts over time.

4. Return to chapters that speak to you. The wisdom of the Tao reveals itself gradually, often in unexpected ways.

Remember, the Tao that can be spoken is not the eternal Tao. This book is not meant to provide definitive answers, but rather to spark your own exploration and awakening. Trust your intuition and let the Tao guide you on your unique path.

May this book serve as a companion on your journey to greater wisdom, peace, and harmony.

In the spirit of the Tao,

Azariah Samuel A.

Chapter 1: Being the Dao

Nameless, yet named,
　　Formless, yet formed,
　　The Dao flows eternal,
　　Through all, unadorned.
　　In silence it speaks,
　　In stillness it moves,
　　The source of all being,
　　Where mystery proves.

Explanation:

The concept of Dao (or Tao) is central to Taoist philosophy, yet it defies simple definition. The opening lines of the Tao Te Ching state, "The Tao that can be told is not the eternal Tao. The name that can be named is not the eternal name." This paradox invites us to look beyond our limited understanding and embrace a deeper, more intuitive knowing.

The Dao represents the fundamental nature of the universe, the underlying principle that gives rise to all existence. It is both immanent (present in all things) and transcendent (beyond all things). The Dao is often described as empty, yet it gives birth to the "ten thousand things" – all the diverse phenomena of the world.

In Taoist thought, the Dao is not a deity or a supreme being, but rather an impersonal force or principle. It operates without intent or effort, following its own nature. This concept is expressed in the principle of wu wei, or "non-action," which we'll explore in later chapters.

The Dao is often compared to water, which flows naturally, taking the path of least resistance. It nourishes all things without discrimination and seeks the lowest places, yet it is essential for all life. This metaphor encourages us to cultivate humility, flexibility, and harmony with our environment.

Understanding the Dao involves moving beyond intellectual knowledge to experiential wisdom. It requires a shift in perception, learning to see the underlying unity behind apparent diversity. This doesn't mean rejecting the world of form, but rather recognizing it as a manifestation of the formless Dao.

The paradoxical nature of the Dao challenges our dualistic thinking. It is both being and non-being, action and non-action, emptiness and fullness. By contemplating these apparent contradictions, we can begin to transcend the limitations of logical thought and tap into a more holistic understanding of reality.

In the Taoist worldview, the Dao is not separate from nature or the material world. Instead, it flows through and animates all things. This perspective fosters a deep reverence for the natural world and an understanding of our interconnectedness with all life. It encourages us to live in harmony with natural cycles and processes, rather than attempting to dominate or control them.

The concept of Dao also relates to the idea of returning to our original nature. In Taoist thought, we are born in alignment with the Dao but gradually lose this connection through socialization and the development of the ego. The spiritual path, then, is not about attaining something new, but rather about rediscovering our innate connection to the Dao.

Modern Application:

In our fast-paced, goal-oriented society, the concept of Dao offers a refreshing perspective. It invites us to slow down, observe, and align ourselves with the natural flow of life. This might involve:

1. Practicing mindfulness to become more aware of the present moment. By cultivating presence, we can tune into the subtle movements of the Dao in our daily lives.

2. Observing natural cycles and rhythms in our environment and our own lives. This could mean paying attention to the changing seasons, the cycles of the moon, or the natural ebb and flow of our energy throughout the day.

3. Letting go of rigid expectations and learning to adapt to changing circumstances. When we resist what is, we create suffering. By accepting and flowing with change, we align ourselves with the Dao.

4. Cultivating a sense of wonder and openness to the mysteries of existence. The Dao reminds us that there is always more to reality than what we can perceive or understand.

5. Recognizing the interconnectedness of all things and acting with compassion. Understanding that we are all manifestations of the Dao can lead to greater empathy and a sense of unity with others and the natural world.

6. Simplifying our lives and letting go of excess. The Dao operates with effortless efficiency. By decluttering our physical spaces and our minds, we create room for the Dao to flow more freely in our lives.

7. Trusting in the natural unfolding of events. While this doesn't mean becoming passive, it does involve recognizing that there is a greater wisdom at work beyond our individual desires and plans.

By "being the Dao," we learn to move through life with greater ease and harmony. We become less attached to outcomes and more attuned to the process. This shift can lead to reduced stress, increased creativity, and a deeper sense of fulfillment.

In practical terms, this might mean:

- Taking time each day for quiet reflection or meditation
- Spending more time in nature, observing and learning from its patterns

- Practicing acceptance of situations we cannot change
- Cultivating patience and trust in the timing of events
- Making decisions based on what feels in alignment with our deepest nature, rather than just following social conventions or expectations

Reflection Questions:

1. How do you experience the Dao in your daily life? Can you recall moments when you felt particularly in flow or in harmony with your surroundings?

2. In what ways do you resist the natural flow of events? How might you cultivate greater acceptance?

3. Reflect on a time when you felt deeply connected to the world around you. What insights did this experience offer?

4. How might your life change if you viewed everything as a manifestation of the Dao? How would it affect your relationships, your work, your self-perception?

5. What practices could you incorporate into your daily routine to help you align more closely with the Dao?

Remember, understanding the Dao is not an intellectual exercise but a lifelong journey of experience and intuition. Be patient with yourself as you explore these concepts, and allow the wisdom to unfold naturally in your life.

Chapter 2: Being the Yin-Yang

Dark and light, in endless dance,
Soft and hard, in balance true,
Yin and yang, two sides of one,
In constant flux, forever new.
Embrace the whole, reject not half,
For wisdom lies in unity,
The sage sees beauty in contrast,
And finds strength in duality.

Explanation:

The concept of yin and yang is fundamental to Taoist philosophy and Chinese thought in general. It represents the duality inherent in all aspects of the universe. Yin and yang are complementary forces that interact to form a dynamic system in which the whole is greater than the sum of its parts.

Traditionally, yin is associated with qualities such as darkness, femininity, passivity, and softness, while yang is associated with light, masculinity, activity, and hardness. However, it's crucial to understand that these associations are not fixed or absolute. Yin and yang are relative terms, always in relationship to each other.

The symbol of yin and yang, known as the taijitu, visually represents this concept. The circle is divided into black and white sections, each containing a small circle of the opposite color. This symbolizes several key principles:

1. Interdependence: Yin and yang are not opposing forces, but complementary aspects of a whole. They depend on each other for definition and existence.

2. Dynamic balance: The boundary between yin and yang is curved, suggesting constant motion and change. This represents the ever-shifting balance between these forces.

3. Mutual transformation: The small circles of opposite colors within each half show that within yin there is yang, and within yang there is yin. Each contains the seed of its opposite.

4. Relativity: What is yin in one relationship might be yang in another. For example, day is yang compared to night, but night is yang compared to twilight.

In Taoist thought, the interplay of yin and yang gives rise to the "ten thousand things" - all the phenomena in the universe. This concept encourages us to see beyond rigid dualities and recognize the interconnectedness and fluidity of all things.

The yin-yang philosophy also teaches us about the nature of change. It suggests that all phenomena are in a constant state of flux, with yin and yang always in the process of becoming each other. This idea is reflected in the I Ching, or Book of Changes, which is closely related to Taoist philosophy.

Understanding yin and yang can help us navigate life's challenges with greater wisdom and equanimity. It reminds us that no situation is entirely good or bad, and that what seems negative often contains the potential for positive transformation, and vice versa.

Modern Application:

In our modern lives, the principle of yin and yang offers valuable insights and practical applications:

1. Embracing balance: In a world that often values yang qualities (action, achievement, extroversion) over yin qualities (rest, reflection, introversion), we can strive for a more balanced approach. This might mean incorporating periods of rest and reflection into our busy schedules, or valuing quiet contemplation as much as active productivity.

2. Accepting change: Understanding the constant interplay of yin and yang can help us accept and adapt to life's changes more gracefully. When we face challenges, we can remember that this difficult period contains the seeds of future growth and opportunity.

3. Holistic problem-solving: Instead of seeing problems in black and white terms, we can look for more nuanced, holistic solutions that address both yin and yang aspects of a situation.

4. Relationship dynamics: In our personal and professional relationships, we can appreciate the complementary strengths that different individuals bring, rather than seeing differences as sources of conflict.

5. Health and wellness: Traditional Chinese Medicine, which is based on Taoist principles, sees health as a state of balance between yin and yang in the body. This holistic approach can complement Western medical practices.

6. Environmental awareness: The yin-yang concept reminds us of the delicate balance in nature and the importance of maintaining harmony in our ecosystems.

7. Personal growth: By recognizing and developing both our yin and yang qualities, we can become more well-rounded individuals. This might involve a typically action-oriented person learning to cultivate stillness, or a naturally introspective person practicing more assertiveness.

8. Conflict resolution: In disagreements, we can look for the valid points on both sides rather than insisting on a single "right" perspective. This can lead to more creative and satisfying resolutions.

Practical steps might include:

- Practicing mindfulness to observe the interplay of opposite qualities in your experiences
- Keeping a journal to reflect on how apparent opposites in your life complement each other

- Engaging in activities that balance your natural tendencies (e.g., meditation for active people, exercise for sedentary people)
- In decision-making, consciously considering both the potential benefits and drawbacks of each option
- Cultivating appreciation for the person or quality that most challenges or frustrates you, recognizing its role in your growth

Reflection Questions:

1. How do you see the interplay of yin and yang in your own life? Can you identify areas where you might need more balance?

2. Reflect on a recent challenge you faced. How might viewing it through the lens of yin and yang offer new perspectives or solutions?

3. In what ways do you resist or deny the "opposite" qualities within yourself? How might embracing these qualities lead to greater wholeness?

4. Think of a person who seems very different from you. How might your qualities complement each other in a yin-yang dynamic?

5. How can you apply the principle of yin and yang to a current goal or project in your life?

Remember, the concept of yin and yang is not about achieving a static, perfect balance, but rather about flowing with the natural rhythms of change and transformation. As you contemplate these ideas, remain open to the ever-shifting dance of opposites in your own experience.

Chapter 3: Being Ziran (Naturalness)

Effortless as falling leaves,
Spontaneous as flowing streams,
In harmony with nature's beat,
Ziran – the way things truly seem.
No need to force, no need to strive,
Just be as you were meant to be,
For in your essence, pure and frcc,
The Tao's perfection you will see.

Explanation:

Ziran (⬦⬦) is a fundamental concept in Taoist philosophy that is often translated as "naturalness," "spontaneity," or "self-so-ness." It refers to the innate character of things as they exist in their natural state, unaltered by human intervention or desire. Ziran embodies the idea that everything in the universe has its own intrinsic nature and follows its own course without external compulsion.

In the Tao Te Ching, Lao Tzu writes, "Man follows the earth. Earth follows the universe. The universe follows the Tao. The Tao follows what is natural." This passage illustrates the Taoist view that the highest wisdom lies in aligning ourselves with the natural order of things, rather than imposing our will upon the world.

The concept of ziran is closely related to wu wei (non-action), which we'll explore in a later chapter. Both principles encourage a way of being that is in harmony with the Tao, free from forced effort or artificial constraints. However, while wu wei focuses on non-interference, ziran emphasizes the inherent authenticity and spontaneity of all things.

Ziran doesn't mean passivity or a return to a primitive state. Rather, it suggests that our truest actions and most authentic expressions arise when we're in touch with our essential nature and the nature of the world around us. It's about allowing things to unfold according to their own intrinsic principles, rather than trying to control or manipulate them based on our limited understanding.

In Taoist thought, ziran is not just a characteristic of the natural world, but also an ideal state for human beings. When we embody ziran, we act in ways that are genuine, spontaneous, and in alignment with our deepest nature. This state is often associated with the innocence and spontaneity of children, who haven't yet learned to suppress their natural impulses or conform to societal expectations.

The principle of ziran also relates to the Taoist understanding of virtue (de). In this context, virtue isn't about adhering to moral rules, but about cultivating and expressing one's innate nature in harmony with the Tao. As we align ourselves more closely with ziran, our actions naturally become more virtuous and beneficial to ourselves and others.

Modern Application:

In our modern world, which often values control, planning, and achievement, the concept of ziran offers a refreshing alternative. Here are some ways we can apply this principle in our daily lives:

1. Self-acceptance: Instead of trying to force ourselves to fit an idealized image, we can practice accepting our natural inclinations, strengths, and limitations. This doesn't mean avoiding growth, but rather allowing our development to unfold organically.

2. Intuitive decision-making: While rational analysis has its place, ziran encourages us to also trust our intuition and natural instincts when making choices.

3. Creativity: By letting go of rigid expectations and allowing ideas to flow naturally, we can tap into a more authentic and spontaneous form of creativity.

4. Parenting and education: Embracing ziran might mean allowing children more freedom to explore and learn according to their own interests and natural rhythms, rather than imposing a one-size-fits-all approach.

5. Career and life purpose: Instead of forcing ourselves into careers that don't align with our true nature, we can seek work that allows us to express our innate talents and passions.

6. Relationships: Practicing ziran in relationships involves being authentic and allowing others to be themselves, rather than trying to change or control them.

7. Problem-solving: Sometimes, allowing a situation to unfold naturally can lead to unexpected solutions that arise organically, rather than through forced intervention.

8. Environmental stewardship: Ziran encourages a more harmonious relationship with nature, working with natural processes rather than against them.

Practical steps might include:

- Practicing mindfulness to become more aware of your natural inclinations and impulses
- Engaging in free-form creative activities without judgment or expectation
- Spending time in nature and observing how natural systems function effortlessly
- Identifying areas of your life where you're expending unnecessary effort and exploring ways to let go
- Practicing spontaneity by occasionally acting on impulse (within reason) rather than always planning everything
- In conversations, allowing yourself to respond naturally rather than always filtering your thoughts

Reflection Questions:

1. In what areas of your life do you feel most natural and spontaneous? How does this state feel different from times when you're forcing things?

2. Reflect on a recent situation where you tried to control an outcome. How might the situation have unfolded differently if you had embraced ziran?

3. What societal expectations or self-imposed rules might be preventing you from expressing your true nature?

4. How can you bring more naturalness and spontaneity into your daily routine?

5. Think of someone you admire for their authenticity. What qualities do they embody that reflect ziran?

Remember, embracing ziran doesn't mean abandoning all structure or responsibility. Instead, it's about finding a way of living that feels more effortless and aligned with your true nature and the natural flow of the universe. As you explore this concept, be patient with yourself and allow your understanding to develop naturally over time.

Chapter 4: Being Wuji (Limitless)

Beyond the bounds of space and time,
> Lies Wuji, vast and undefined,
> No form, no shape, no start or end,
> The primal void where all transcend.
> From emptiness, all things arise,
> In boundlessness, potential lies,
> Embrace the infinite within,
> Where limits fade and Tao begins.

Explanation:

Wuji (◇◇) is a profound concept in Taoist philosophy that can be translated as "limitless," "boundless," or "infinite." It represents the primordial state of the universe before the emergence of yin and yang, a state of undifferentiated potential from which all things arise. In Taoist cosmology, Wuji is often depicted as an empty circle, symbolizing the void or emptiness that precedes creation. This emptiness, however, is not a mere absence or nothingness, but rather a state of unlimited possibility. It is from this state of Wuji that Taiji (the supreme ultimate) emerges, giving rise to yin and yang and subsequently to all phenomena in the universe. The concept of Wuji challenges our ordinary understanding of reality. It points to a dimension beyond duality, beyond the distinctions of being and non-being, form and formlessness. It is the ground of all existence, yet it transcends existence itself. In this sense, Wuji is closely related to the Tao, which is described in the Tao Te Ching as "empty yet inexhaustible."

Understanding Wuji involves a shift in perception, moving beyond our usual conceptual frameworks to glimpse the boundless nature of reality. It invites us to recognize that beneath the apparent diversity and complexity of the world, there is an underlying unity and simplicity. In Taoist spiritual practice, cultivating an awareness of Wuji can lead to profound states of consciousness. By letting go of all mental constructs and returning to a state of primordial openness, one can experience a sense of vastness and freedom beyond ordinary perception. The principle of Wuji also has implications for understanding the nature of the self. From this perspective, our true nature is not limited to our individual identity or personal history, but is fundamentally boundless and interconnected with all of existence.

Modern Application:

While the concept of Wuji may seem abstract, it offers valuable insights that we can apply in our daily lives:

1. Cultivating openness: By recognizing the limitless potential inherent in each moment, we can approach life with greater openness and creativity. This might involve letting go of preconceptions and being more receptive to new ideas and experiences.

2. Embracing uncertainty: The idea of Wuji reminds us that the future is not fixed but full of unlimited possibilities. This can help us navigate uncertainty with greater ease and optimism.

3. Transcending limitations: When we connect with the boundless aspect of our nature, we can move beyond self-imposed limitations and tap into greater potential in various areas of our lives.

4. Problem-solving: Approaching challenges from a state of Wuji-like openness can lead to more innovative and holistic solutions, as we're not constrained by habitual patterns of thinking.

5. Meditation and mindfulness: Practices that cultivate a sense of spacious awareness can help us experience the quality of Wuji in our own consciousness.

6. Creativity: Artists and innovators can draw inspiration from the concept of Wuji, allowing ideas to emerge from a place of boundless potential rather than forcing creativity.

7. Personal growth: Recognizing our essential boundlessness can foster a sense of connection with others and the world around us, leading to greater compassion and a expanded sense of self.

8. Stress reduction: By connecting with the limitless aspect of our being, we can gain perspective on our problems and find a sense of calm amidst life's challenges.

Practical steps might include:

- Practicing open awareness meditation, allowing thoughts and sensations to arise and pass without fixation
- Engaging in creative exercises that encourage free association and unrestricted expression
- Spending time in vast natural spaces to evoke a sense of boundlessness
- Exploring practices like floatation tanks or sky gazing that can induce experiences of expansiveness
- Regularly questioning and releasing limiting beliefs about yourself and what's possible
- Cultivating moments of "beginner's mind" in daily activities, approaching familiar situations with fresh perspective

Reflection Questions:

1. Can you recall a moment when you felt a sense of boundlessness or connection with something greater than yourself? How did this experience affect you?

2. In what areas of your life do you feel most limited? How might the concept of Wuji help you

approach these limitations differently?

3. How does the idea of limitless potential change your perspective on your current goals and aspirations?

4. Reflect on a current challenge in your life. How might approaching it from a state of open, boundless awareness change your response?

5. In what ways do you impose unnecessary limits on your thinking or behavior? How can you practice more openness in your daily life?

Remember, the concept of Wuji is not something to be grasped intellectually, but rather a quality of being to be experienced and embodied. As you contemplate these ideas, allow yourself to rest in the spaciousness of not-knowing, opening to the vast potential that exists in each moment.

Chapter 5: Being Wu Wei (Non-action)

Effortless action, nature's way,
> Wu Wei, the path of least display,
> Not passive, idle, or inert,
> But flow that leaves the world unhurt.
> Like water carving canyons deep,
> Or wind that makes the willows weep,
> In harmony with Tao's design,
> We act, yet leave no forced outline.

Explanation:

Wu Wei (◇◇) is one of the most central and perhaps misunderstood concepts in Taoist philosophy. Often translated as "non-action" or "non-doing," Wu Wei doesn't imply passivity or inertia. Rather, it suggests a way of being and acting that is in perfect harmony with the natural flow of the Tao. The principle of Wu Wei encourages us to act without forcing, striving, or interfering with the natural order of things. It's about aligning our actions with the inherent patterns and rhythms of nature, allowing things to unfold organically rather than imposing our will upon them.

In the Tao Te Ching, Lao Tzu often uses natural metaphors to illustrate Wu Wei. Water, for instance, exemplifies this principle: it flows effortlessly around obstacles, takes the path of least resistance, and yet over time can carve canyons and shape landscapes. Similarly, the sage who embodies Wu Wei accomplishes much without seeming to do anything at all.

Wu Wei is closely related to the concept of ziran (naturalness) that we explored in the previous chapter. While ziran refers to the inherent nature of things, Wu Wei is about how we act in accordance with this nature. When we practice Wu Wei, our actions arise spontaneously from our alignment with the Tao, rather than from ego-driven desires or societal expectations.

It's important to note that Wu Wei doesn't mean doing nothing at all. Rather, it suggests acting without attachment to the outcome, without forcing things against their nature, and without leaving traces of ego-driven effort. It's a state of responsive and responsible action that flows naturally from our understanding of the situation at hand. In Taoist thought, Wu Wei is seen as the most effective way of accomplishing things. By aligning ourselves with the natural flow of events, we can achieve our aims with minimal resistance and maximum efficiency. This idea is expressed in the Taoist phrase "wei wu wei" - doing without doing.

Modern Application:

The principle of Wu Wei offers valuable guidance for navigating our complex modern world:

1. Stress reduction: By letting go of the need to control every aspect of our lives and learning to flow with circumstances, we can significantly reduce stress and anxiety.

2. Leadership: A leader who embodies Wu Wei doesn't micromanage or force their will upon others, but rather creates conditions that allow people to flourish naturally.

3. Problem-solving: Instead of immediately reacting to problems, Wu Wei encourages us to observe and understand the situation fully before taking action. Often, this leads to more elegant and effective solutions.

4. Relationships: Practicing Wu Wei in relationships means allowing others to be as they are, rather than trying to change or control them. This can lead to more harmonious and authentic connections.

5. Creativity: By letting go of forced effort and allowing ideas to arise naturally, we can tap into a more authentic and flowing state of creativity.

6. Time management: Wu Wei doesn't mean procrastination, but rather doing things at the right time and in the right way, which can actually increase productivity.

7. Environmental stewardship: Applying Wu Wei to our interaction with nature means working with natural processes rather than against them, leading to more sustainable practices.

8. Personal growth: Instead of forcing ourselves to change through sheer willpower, Wu Wei suggests creating the right conditions for natural growth and transformation.

Practical steps might include:

- Practicing mindfulness to become more aware of the natural flow of events in your life
- Before taking action, pausing to sense what feels most natural and effortless in the situation
- Identifying areas in your life where you're expending unnecessary effort and exploring ways to let go
- Observing nature and learning from its effortless efficiency
- In conversations, practicing active listening without immediately jumping in to fix or advise
- Experimenting with allowing your day to unfold naturally without rigid planning (when appropriate)
- In physical activities, focusing on relaxation and flow rather than forcing or straining

Reflection Questions:

1. Reflect on a time when you achieved something significant without feeling like you were forcing it. What allowed for this state of effortless action?

2. In what areas of your life do you find yourself struggling or pushing against the natural flow of things? How might you apply Wu Wei in these situations?

3. How does the idea of "doing without doing" challenge your usual approach to accomplishing tasks or achieving goals?

4. Think of someone you know who seems to embody Wu Wei. What qualities do they exhibit that you might cultivate in yourself?

5. How might practicing Wu Wei change your relationship with success and failure?

Remember, Wu Wei is not something to be achieved through effort, as that would contradict its very nature. Instead, it's a state that arises naturally as we align ourselves more closely with the Tao. As you explore this principle, be patient with yourself and allow your understanding to deepen gradually through experience and observation.

Chapter 6: Being Yijing (Creative Change)

In flux and flow, the world revolves,
As Yijing's wisdom evolves,
Through change, the Tao reveals its face,
In every shift, find growth and grace.
Embrace the dance of yin and yang,
Let go of old, let new expand,
For in the cycles of all things,
The sage finds joy that change can bring.

Explanation:

Yijing (◇◇), often known in the West as the I Ching or "Book of Changes," is one of the oldest Chinese classic texts and a fundamental part of Taoist philosophy. While it's a complex system of divination, at its core, Yijing embodies the principle of creative change that permeates the Taoist worldview.

The concept of Yijing recognizes that change is the only constant in the universe. Everything is in a perpetual state of transformation, shifting between yin and yang, between various states of being. This constant flux is not random but follows certain patterns and principles that can be observed and understood.

In Taoist thought, change is not something to be feared or resisted, but rather a natural and necessary part of existence. It's through change that growth, renewal, and creativity occur. The sage, according to this view, is one who can flow with these changes, understanding their rhythms and adapting harmoniously to them.

The Yijing presents a model of reality composed of 64 hexagrams, each representing a particular state or situation. These hexagrams are made up of solid and broken lines, symbolizing yang and yin energies respectively. The shifting of these lines demonstrates how one state transforms into another, illustrating the dynamic interplay of forces in the universe.

Key to the Yijing's philosophy is the idea that within each situation lies the seed of its transformation. In other words, change is not just external but inherent in the nature of things. This perspective encourages a proactive and creative approach to life, where we participate in shaping our circumstances rather than being passive recipients of fate.

The Yijing also emphasizes the importance of timing. Just as there are seasons in nature, there are appropriate times for action and times for restraint in human affairs. The wise person, attuned to these cycles, knows when to advance and when to retreat, when to speak and when to remain silent.

Modern Application:

The wisdom of Yijing offers valuable insights for navigating our rapidly changing modern world:

1. Adaptability: In an era of fast-paced technological and social change, cultivating the ability to adapt flexibly to new situations is crucial.

2. Decision-making: The Yijing encourages a holistic approach to decision-making, considering multiple perspectives and potential outcomes.

3. Resilience: Understanding that change is constant can help us bounce back from setbacks, seeing them as natural parts of life's cycles rather than permanent defeats.

4. Innovation: Embracing change fosters a mindset of creativity and innovation, essential in many fields of work and personal growth.

5. Relationships: Recognizing that people and relationships naturally evolve over time can lead to more understanding and less conflict in our interactions.

6. Personal growth: Viewing our personal development as a continual process of transformation aligns with the Yijing's philosophy of constant change.

7. Business strategy: In the business world, the Yijing's principles can inform adaptive strategies that respond creatively to changing market conditions.

8. Environmental awareness: Understanding the interconnected and ever-changing nature of ecosystems can inform more sustainable environmental practices.

Practical steps might include:

- Practicing mindfulness to become more aware of the constant changes in your thoughts, emotions, and surroundings
- Journaling about how you've changed over time, noting patterns and cycles in your life
- When facing a decision, consider multiple perspectives and potential outcomes, as suggested by the Yijing
- Cultivating flexibility in your daily routines, occasionally introducing changes to keep yourself adaptable
- In times of difficulty, reflect on how this situation might be laying the groundwork for future positive changes
- Regularly reassessing your goals and plans, being willing to adjust them in response to changing circumstances
- Studying natural cycles (seasons, moon phases, tides) to deepen your understanding of change patterns

Reflection Questions:

1. Think of a major change in your life. How did you initially react to it, and how do you view it now with hindsight?

2. In what areas of your life do you resist change? How might embracing change in these areas lead to growth or new opportunities?

3. Reflect on a current challenge you're facing. What potential for positive transformation might be hidden within this situation?

4. How does the idea that "change is the only constant" affect your approach to long-term planning and goal-setting?

5. Can you identify any recurring cycles or patterns in your life? How might awareness of these patterns help you navigate future changes?

Remember, the wisdom of Yijing is not about predicting the future, but about understanding the nature of change itself. As you contemplate these ideas, try to cultivate a sense of flexibility and openness to the ever-changing flow of life. Embrace change not as a disruption, but as the very essence of existence, full of potential for growth and new beginnings.

Chapter 7: Being Wu Xin (No Ego)

Letting go of self, we find
>The boundless Tao, no "me" or "mine"
>Wu Xin, the state of no-mind's grace
>Where ego's shadow leaves no trace
>In stillness, true self shines so bright
>Unbound by thought, pure as light
>The sage, in selflessness complete
>Finds wisdom in ego's retreat

Explanation:

Wu Xin (◇◇), often translated as "no-mind" or "no ego," is a profound concept in Taoist philosophy that points to a state of being free from the constraints of the ego-self. It's not about erasing the self entirely, but rather transcending the limited, conceptual idea of self that often dominates our experience.

In Taoist thought, the ego – our sense of a separate, fixed self – is seen as a construct that obscures our true nature and our connection to the Tao. This ego-self is characterized by desires, fears, judgments, and attachments that create suffering and separation. Wu Xin represents a state of consciousness where these egoic patterns fall away, revealing a more expansive and interconnected sense of being.

The term "Wu Xin" literally means "no heart-mind," where "heart-mind" (xin) in Chinese philosophy refers to the seat of both thought and emotion. Thus, Wu Xin suggests a state beyond ordinary thinking and feeling, a direct, unmediated experience of reality.

This concept is closely related to the Buddhist idea of "no-self" or "emptiness," but in Taoism, it's seen more as a return to our original nature rather than an achievement or attainment. It's the natural state of being when we're not caught up in the stories and dramas of the ego.

In the Tao Te Ching, Lao Tzu often speaks of the virtues of emptiness, humility, and non-attachment – all qualities that reflect the state of Wu Xin. The sage, in this view, is one who has let go of personal ambition and self-importance, acting from a place of spontaneous wisdom rather than ego-driven motivations.

Importantly, Wu Xin doesn't mean becoming a blank slate or losing one's individuality. Rather, it allows for a more authentic expression of our true nature, unencumbered by the fears and desires of the ego. In this state, we can respond to life more freely and compassionately, without the constant need to protect or enhance our self-image.

Modern Application:

The concept of Wu Xin offers valuable insights for our modern lives, where ego-driven behaviors often lead to stress, conflict, and dissatisfaction:

1. Stress Reduction: By learning to detach from our egoic thought patterns, we can find greater peace and equanimity in the face of life's challenges.

2. Improved Relationships: When we're less caught up in defending our ego, we can listen more deeply to others and respond with greater empathy and understanding.

3. Creativity: Many artists and innovators report that their best ideas come when they're in a state of "flow" – a concept very similar to Wu Xin. By letting go of self-consciousness, we can tap into greater creativity.

4. Decision Making: Without the ego's constant need for validation and security, we can make decisions more clearly, based on what's truly needed in a situation rather than what will make us look good.

5. Leadership: Leaders who embody Wu Xin can inspire and guide others without the need for personal glory or power, creating more collaborative and effective teams.

6. Personal Growth: Recognizing the constructs of our ego allows us to work with our patterns more effectively, leading to genuine transformation rather than surface-level changes.

7. Spiritual Practice: Wu Xin is both a goal and a method in many spiritual traditions. Cultivating this state can deepen our spiritual experiences and insights.

8. Environmental Awareness: As we let go of our sense of separate self, we naturally feel more connected to the world around us, which can inspire more environmentally conscious behavior.

Practical steps might include:

- Practicing mindfulness meditation to observe thoughts and emotions without identifying with them
- Engaging in activities that induce a state of flow, where self-consciousness fades away
- Regularly reflecting on your motivations: are they coming from ego or from a deeper place?
- Practicing humility and anonymity in good deeds, doing things without seeking recognition
- When in conflict, try to see the situation from the other person's perspective, letting go of the need to be right
- Spending time in nature to experience a sense of connection beyond the individual self
- Engaging in selfless service or volunteer work, acting for the benefit of others without personal gain

Reflection Questions:

1. Can you recall a moment when you felt completely free of self-consciousness? What was that experience like?

2. In what areas of your life does your ego feel most prominent or protective? How might letting go in these areas change your experience?

3. How does the idea of "no ego" challenge your current understanding of personal growth and success?

4. Reflect on a recent conflict or disagreement. How might it have unfolded differently if you had approached it from a state of Wu Xin?

5. What fears or attachments might be preventing you from experiencing a greater sense of egolessness in your daily life?

Remember, Wu Xin is not about suppressing or fighting against the ego, but rather about seeing through its illusions and allowing a more expansive sense of self to emerge naturally. As you explore this concept, be patient and compassionate with yourself. The journey towards Wu Xin is not about achieving a perfect state, but about gradually loosening the grip of ego and opening to the boundless nature of your true self.

Chapter 8: Being Zhuangzi's Flow

Like fish in streams, so free and light,
Or birds in flight at dawn's first light,
Zhuangzi's flow, a state sublime,
Where self and action both align.
No thought of gain, no fear of loss,
Just being here, all boundaries crossed.
In perfect ease, the sage resides,
As life's great river gently glides.

Explanation:

Zhuangzi, one of the foundational figures of Taoism alongside Lao Tzu, offers a unique perspective on living in harmony with the Tao. His philosophy, often expressed through colorful parables and paradoxical statements, emphasizes a state of being that we might call "flow" – a spontaneous, effortless alignment with the natural course of things.

Zhuangzi's concept of flow goes beyond mere relaxation or passivity. It's a state of heightened awareness and responsiveness, where our actions arise naturally from our attunement to the present moment and the broader context of the Tao. In this state, the boundaries between self and other, subject and object, begin to dissolve.

One of Zhuangzi's most famous parables illustrates this idea. He describes a skilled butcher who never needs to sharpen his knife because he has learned to move with the natural lines and spaces within the animal's body. This story isn't just about physical skill, but about a way of being that is so in tune with the inherent nature of things that action becomes effortless and perfectly appropriate.

Zhuangzi emphasizes the limitations of human knowledge and the often arbitrary nature of social conventions. He encourages us to let go of rigid categorizations and judgments, and instead to embrace a more fluid, open-ended approach to life. This doesn't mean abandoning all structure or ethics, but rather holding our concepts lightly and remaining open to the ever-changing nature of reality.

Another key aspect of Zhuangzi's philosophy is the idea of "free and easy wandering" (xiaoyao you). This refers to a state of spiritual freedom where one is no longer bound by social conventions, personal ambitions, or even the fear of death. It's a way of moving through life with ease and joy, responding spontaneously to each situation without being weighed down by preconceptions or attachments.

Zhuangzi also introduces the concept of "skillful means" or "spontaneous action" (wu wei), which aligns closely with the idea of flow. This is not about following a set of rules or techniques, but about cultivating a state of being where appropriate action arises naturally and effortlessly in response to each unique situation.

Modern Application:

Zhuangzi's ideas about flow offer valuable insights for navigating our complex modern lives:

1. Work and Productivity: Instead of forcing ourselves to be productive, we can learn to align our efforts with our natural rhythms and inclinations, leading to more effortless and effective work.

2. Creativity: By letting go of preconceptions and allowing ideas to arise spontaneously, we can tap into deeper wells of creativity and innovation.

3. Stress Management: Embracing Zhuangzi's "free and easy wandering" can help us maintain equanimity in the face of life's challenges, reducing stress and anxiety.

4. Decision Making: Rather than agonizing over decisions, we can cultivate the ability to respond spontaneously and appropriately to each situation as it arises.

5. Relationships: By letting go of fixed expectations and judgments, we can engage with others more openly and authentically, allowing relationships to unfold naturally.

6. Learning and Skill Development: Zhuangzi's butcher parable suggests that true mastery comes not from rigid practice, but from deep attunement to the nature of what we're working with.

7. Adaptability: In a rapidly changing world, cultivating the ability to flow with circumstances rather than resist them can be a crucial skill.

8. Self-Acceptance: Zhuangzi's philosophy encourages us to embrace our authentic nature rather than constantly trying to conform to external standards.

Practical steps might include:

- Practicing mindfulness to develop greater awareness of the present moment
- Engaging in improvisational activities (music, dance, theater) to cultivate spontaneity
- Regularly stepping outside your comfort zone to challenge fixed patterns of thinking and behaving
- Spending time in nature, observing how natural systems flow and adapt
- When faced with a challenge, asking "What would this look like if it were easy?" to shift into a more flow-like state
- Experimenting with following your natural rhythms of energy and creativity rather than adhering to a rigid schedule
- Practicing acceptance of things as they are, rather than always trying to change or control them

Reflection Questions:

1. Can you recall a time when you experienced a state of flow? What were you doing, and how did it feel?

2. In what areas of your life do you feel most "stuck" or resistant? How might adopting a more flow-like approach change these situations?

3. How does the idea of "free and easy wandering" challenge or support your current life goals and ambitions?

4. Reflect on a skill you've mastered or are working to master. How might Zhuangzi's butcher parable apply to your approach to this skill?

5. In what ways do social conventions or self-imposed rules limit your spontaneity and authenticity? How might you begin to loosen these constraints?

Remember, Zhuangzi's philosophy isn't about achieving a perfect state of flow, but about cultivating a more flexible, spontaneous approach to life. As you explore these ideas, allow yourself to play and experiment, embracing the unexpected and finding joy in the ever-changing flow of existence.

Chapter 9: Being De (Virtue)

Not moral codes or rigid rules,
>But inner power, wisdom's jewels,
>De flows from Tao, a force unseen,
>In harmony, our actions gleam.
>No need to preach or to proclaim,
>True virtue seeks no praise or fame,
>Like water nourishing the land,
>De works its magic, soft and grand.

Explanation:

De (德), often translated as "virtue" or "power," is a central concept in Taoist philosophy that goes far beyond conventional notions of morality or goodness. In Taoist thought, De represents the innate power that arises from one's alignment with the Tao. It's not a set of external rules or behaviors, but rather an expression of one's true nature in harmony with the fundamental principles of the universe.

The character 德 (De) is composed of two parts: 直 (zhi), meaning "straight" or "upright," and 心 (xin), meaning "heart" or "mind." This suggests that De is about a kind of inner straightness or integrity, a natural expression of one's deepest nature rather than conformity to external standards.

In the Tao Te Ching, Lao Tzu often describes De as a kind of potency or efficacy that comes from being in accord with the Tao. It's the power that allows things to be what they are and to fulfill their nature. For humans, cultivating De means aligning ourselves with the Tao and allowing our actions to flow naturally from this alignment.

Importantly, De is not something we achieve through striving or effort. Rather, it's our original nature, often obscured by societal conditioning and ego-driven desires. The cultivation of De, therefore, is more about removing obstacles and returning to our authentic selves than about adding something new.

Lao Tzu often uses natural metaphors to illustrate the quality of De. For instance, he compares it to water, which nourishes all things without contention, always seeking the lowest place. This image conveys the humble, yielding, yet powerfully beneficial nature of true virtue.

Another key aspect of De is its effortless influence. Someone embodying De doesn't need to impose their will on others or preach about morality. Instead, their very presence and actions naturally influence those around them in a positive way, like a pebble creating ripples in a pond.

Modern Application:

The Taoist concept of De offers valuable insights for personal growth and ethical living in our modern world:

1. Authenticity: Rather than trying to conform to external standards of goodness, we can focus on expressing our authentic selves in alignment with deeper principles.

2. Leadership: Leaders who embody De inspire others through their actions and presence, rather than through force or manipulation.

3. Ethics: Instead of following rigid moral codes, we can cultivate an innate sense of rightness that responds flexibly to each unique situation.

4. Personal Power: By aligning with the Tao, we can tap into a source of inner strength and effectiveness that doesn't rely on external validation or resources.

5. Influence: We can learn to positively impact others not through preaching or persuasion, but through the natural influence of our aligned actions.

6. Environmental Stewardship: Understanding De can inspire a more harmonious relationship with nature, where we support the inherent qualities and processes of natural systems.

7. Conflict Resolution: Approaching conflicts with the spirit of De can lead to more harmonious resolutions that honor the nature of all involved.

8. Self-Cultivation: Focusing on De shifts our approach to personal growth from acquisition of virtues to removal of obstacles to our innate nature.

Practical steps might include:

- Practicing self-reflection to become more aware of your authentic impulses versus conditioned responses
- Cultivating mindfulness to stay attuned to the present moment and respond naturally to what arises
- When faced with ethical decisions, quieting the mind and listening for the response that feels most aligned with your deepest nature
- Observing the natural world and learning from how it embodies effortless virtue
- In leadership or parenting roles, focusing on setting a good example rather than imposing rules
- Practicing acts of anonymous kindness, cultivating virtue without seeking recognition
- Regularly reassessing your actions and motivations: do they flow naturally from your authentic self, or are they driven by ego or social pressure?

Reflection Questions:

1. Reflect on a time when you acted in a way that felt completely natural and right. How did this differ from times when you were trying to be "good" based on external standards?

2. In what areas of your life do you feel most authentic and aligned? Where do you feel most out of alignment?

3. How does the concept of De challenge or support your current understanding of ethics and morality?

4. Think of someone you know who seems to embody De. What qualities do they exhibit, and how do they influence others?

5. How might embracing the concept of De change your approach to personal growth or self-improvement?

Remember, cultivating De is not about striving for perfection or adhering to a set of rules. It's about gradually aligning ourselves with the Tao and allowing our innate virtue to express itself naturally. As you explore this concept, be patient with yourself and trust in the wisdom of your deeper nature. The path of De is one of unfolding and returning, rather than achieving or acquiring.

Chapter 10: Being Yi (Unity)

In the dance of many, find the One,

    Where separation's illusion is undone,

    Yi, the unity that binds us all,

    In Tao's embrace, no barrier, no wall.

    From stars to atoms, one grand design,

    In you, in me, the cosmos intertwine,

    The sage sees oneness in every face,

    And moves through life with fluid grace.

Explanation:

Yi (◈), meaning "one" or "unity," is a fundamental concept in Taoist philosophy that points to the underlying oneness of all existence. This idea of unity is not just an abstract philosophical concept, but a profound truth about the nature of reality that has far-reaching implications for how we live and perceive the world.

In Taoist thought, while the world appears to be composed of myriad separate entities, this diversity is understood as a manifestation of a single, unified Tao. The apparent separation between things is seen as an illusion created by our limited perception. Just as waves are not separate from the ocean, all phenomena are expressions of the one underlying reality.

The Tao Te Ching often alludes to this unity, speaking of returning to the One or recognizing the common source of all things. This perspective sees the universe not as a collection of isolated parts, but as an interconnected whole where each part influences and is influenced by every other part.

Understanding Yi involves a shift in perception from fragmentation to wholeness. It's about recognizing that the boundaries we perceive between self and other, mind and body, humanity and nature, are mental constructs rather than absolute realities. This doesn't negate the relative truth of our everyday experience of separation, but it points to a deeper truth of fundamental interconnectedness.

The concept of Yi also relates to the idea of non-duality. While the world of form is characterized by apparent opposites (yin and yang, light and dark, good and bad), from the perspective of Yi, these opposites are seen as complementary aspects of a greater whole rather than truly separate or conflicting forces.

For the Taoist sage, realizing Yi leads to a profound sense of harmony and compassion. When we truly understand that we are not separate from others or from the world around us, our actions naturally become more considerate and holistic. This understanding dissolves the root of conflict and competition, replacing it with a sense of cooperation and mutual support.

Modern Application:

The concept of Yi offers valuable insights for navigating our increasingly interconnected yet often divided modern world:

1. Environmental Awareness: Recognizing our fundamental unity with nature can inspire more sustainable and respectful environmental practices.

2. Conflict Resolution: Understanding our essential oneness can help us approach conflicts with empathy and seek win-win solutions rather than adversarial outcomes.

3. Social Justice: The realization of unity undermines the basis for discrimination and promotes equality and inclusivity.

4. Mental Health: Recognizing our connection to a larger whole can alleviate feelings of isolation and contribute to a sense of belonging and purpose.

5. Creativity and Innovation: Seeing the interconnections between seemingly disparate fields can lead to novel insights and creative solutions.

6. Teamwork and Collaboration: In work environments, fostering a sense of unity can enhance cooperation and synergy within teams.

7. Personal Relationships: Understanding Yi can deepen our connections with others, promoting empathy and compassion in our interactions.

8. Holistic Health: Recognizing the unity of mind and body encourages a more integrated approach to health and wellness.

Practical steps might include:

- Practicing meditation or mindfulness to experience the interconnectedness of all phenomena
- Engaging in activities that foster a sense of connection with nature, such as hiking or gardening
- Cultivating empathy by regularly considering situations from others' perspectives
- Exploring systems thinking to understand the complex interconnections in various fields
- Participating in community service or collaborative projects to experience unity in action
- Studying ecology or quantum physics to gain scientific insights into the interconnected nature of reality
- Practicing loving-kindness meditation to extend a sense of unity and compassion to all beings

Reflection Questions:

1. Can you recall a moment when you felt a deep sense of connection or unity with something beyond yourself? How did this experience affect you?

2. How might your life and actions change if you constantly remembered your fundamental unity with all things?

3. In what areas of your life do you feel most separate or isolated? How could the understanding of Yi transform these experiences?

4. Reflect on a current conflict or disagreement in your life. How might approaching it from a perspective of unity change the situation?

5. How does the concept of Yi challenge or support your current worldview and beliefs?

Remember, the realization of Yi is not about erasing all distinctions or denying the relative reality of our everyday experience. Rather, it's about recognizing a deeper truth of interconnectedness that underlies the apparent diversity of the world. As you contemplate these ideas, allow yourself to softly shift between the perspective of separation and unity, gradually integrating both into a more comprehensive understanding of reality.

Chapter 11: Being from Wu (Emptiness)

From emptiness, all forms arise,
    In nothingness, potential lies,
    Wu, the void that's full of all,
    Where boundaries fade, and barriers fall.
    Not lack or loss, but space to be,
    The womb of possibility,
    The sage, embracing emptiness,
    Finds fullness in Wu's gentle caress.

Explanation:

Wu (◈), often translated as "emptiness" or "nothingness," is a profound and paradoxical concept in Taoist philosophy. Far from being a mere absence or lack, Wu represents the unlimited potential from which all things arise. It's the formless ground of being that gives birth to the "ten thousand things" of manifested reality.

In the Tao Te Ching, Lao Tzu uses several metaphors to illustrate the nature and importance of Wu:

"We put thirty spokes together and call it a wheel;

But it is on the space where there is nothing that the usefulness of the wheel depends.

We turn clay to make a vessel;

But it is on the space where there is nothing that the usefulness of the vessel depends.

We pierce doors and windows to make a house;

And it is on these spaces where there is nothing that the usefulness of the house depends.

Therefore just as we take advantage of what is, we should recognize the usefulness of what is not."

This passage highlights that it's the empty space – the Wu – that gives functionality and purpose to physical objects. Similarly, in our lives and in the universe at large, it's the underlying emptiness that allows for movement, change, and the emergence of new forms.

Wu is closely related to the Taoist concept of Wuji, the primordial state of undifferentiated potential that precedes the emergence of Yin and Yang. It's a state of limitless possibility, unbound by form or definition. In this sense, Wu is not a negation of existence, but rather the very source of all existence.

The idea of Wu challenges our usual way of thinking, which tends to focus on tangible, defined things. It invites us to shift our attention to the spaces between, the pauses, the moments of non-doing. In these apparent voids, we may find a profound richness and potential.

For the Taoist sage, cultivating an understanding of Wu leads to a state of openness and receptivity. By emptying oneself of fixed notions and ego-driven desires, one becomes capable of responding flexibly and appropriately to each unique situation. This emptiness is not a blank state, but a state of alert receptivity, like an empty cup ready to be filled.

Modern Application:

The concept of Wu offers valuable insights for our modern lives:

1. Creativity: Understanding Wu can enhance creativity by helping us appreciate the potential in apparent "nothingness" and allowing new ideas to emerge from a space of open possibility.

2. Stress Reduction: Embracing emptiness can help reduce mental clutter and create space for relaxation and rejuvenation.

3. Problem Solving: Sometimes, the solution to a problem lies not in adding more, but in creating space – stepping back to see the bigger picture.

4. Personal Growth: Letting go of fixed self-concepts (emptying the self) can open up new possibilities for growth and transformation.

5. Time Management: Recognizing the value of "empty" time can lead to more balanced and effective use of our time, including the importance of rest and reflection.

6. Minimalism: Wu aligns with minimalist philosophies, encouraging us to appreciate simplicity and find value in less.

7. Meditation and Mindfulness: Many meditation practices involve cultivating a state of empty, open awareness, aligning with the Taoist concept of Wu.

8. Innovation: In fields like design and technology, the concept of Wu can inspire solutions that make effective use of space and simplicity.

Practical steps might include:

- Practicing meditation, particularly techniques that cultivate open awareness
- Decluttering your physical space to create room for new possibilities
- Incorporating pauses or moments of stillness into your daily routine
- When problem-solving, try "emptying your mind" of preconceptions before approaching the issue
- Experimenting with fasting or digital detoxes to experience the potential in "emptiness"
- In creative endeavors, start with a blank canvas (literal or metaphorical) and allow ideas to emerge
- Practice listening to others with an "empty" mind, free from preconceptions or the need to respond

Reflection Questions:

1. Recall a time when you experienced a sense of emptiness or void in your life. In hindsight, what potential or possibilities were present in that space?

2. How might embracing the concept of Wu change your approach to challenges or obstacles in your life?

3. In what areas of your life do you feel overwhelmed or cluttered? How could creating more "empty space" in these areas be beneficial?

4. How does the idea that emptiness is the source of all things challenge or support your current worldview?

5. Reflect on the spaces or pauses in your daily life. How might you more fully appreciate and utilize these moments of "emptiness"?

Remember, the concept of Wu is not about achieving a state of absolute emptiness or negating the value of form and substance. Rather, it's about recognizing the dynamic interplay between form and emptiness, and appreciating the vast potential that lies in the apparent void. As you explore this concept, allow yourself to become comfortable with not-knowing, with silence, with space – for it is from this emptiness that all possibilities arise.

Chapter 12: Being with Xin (Inner Heart)

Deep within, a sacred space,
Where truth and wisdom interlace,
Xin, the heart-mind's gentle glow,
Guiding us through ebb and flow.
Not just feeling, not just thought,
But where the Tao is truly sought,
The sage, attuned to inner light,
Moves through life with clear insight.

Explanation:

Xin (◈), often translated as "heart-mind," is a fundamental concept in Chinese philosophy, including Taoism. Unlike the Western tendency to separate the heart (emotions) from the mind (intellect), the Chinese concept of Xin integrates both, recognizing them as aspects of a unified center of human consciousness and spirit.

In Taoist thought, Xin is not just an organ or a set of functions, but the very core of our being. It's the place where our deepest intuitions, our true nature, and our connection to the Tao reside. The Xin is seen as the seat of both thinking and feeling, the source of our intentions, and the center of our spiritual awareness.

The character ◈ (Xin) is a pictograph resembling a heart, emphasizing its connection to our innermost essence. In classical Chinese texts, including Taoist works, Xin is often described as the ruler of the body, guiding our actions and responses to the world around us.

For Taoists, cultivating and harmonizing the Xin is crucial for aligning oneself with the Tao. This involves more than just emotional regulation or clear thinking – it's about nurturing a state of receptivity and responsiveness that allows us to move in harmony with the natural flow of life.

The Xin in its ideal state is often described as "empty" or "tranquil." This doesn't mean devoid of thought or feeling, but rather free from fixations, excessive desires, and rigid concepts that obstruct our connection to the Tao. When the Xin is clear and open, it becomes a mirror that accurately reflects reality without distortion.

In the Tao Te Ching, Lao Tzu often speaks of returning to a state of simplicity and naturalness. This can be understood as a return to the original purity of the Xin, unburdened by societal conditioning and ego-driven concerns. From this state, our actions flow spontaneously and appropriately in response to each unique situation.

Modern Application:

The concept of Xin offers valuable insights for our modern lives:

1. Emotional Intelligence: Understanding Xin can help us integrate our emotional and cognitive processes, leading to more balanced decision-making and interactions.

2. Mindfulness: Practices that cultivate awareness of our inner state align with the Taoist emphasis on harmonizing the Xin.

3. Authentic Living: By connecting with our Xin, we can live more authentically, guided by our true nature rather than external pressures or expectations.

4. Stress Management: Learning to return to the tranquility of Xin can be a powerful tool for managing stress and maintaining inner peace.

5. Creativity: Accessing the integrated wisdom of Xin can enhance creativity by allowing intuition and reason to work together seamlessly.

6. Relationships: A clear and open Xin allows for more genuine and compassionate connections with others.

7. Leadership: Leaders who operate from a harmonized Xin can make decisions that are both wise and empathetic.

8. Personal Growth: Cultivating Xin aligns with many approaches to personal development that emphasize self-awareness and inner transformation.

Practical steps might include:

- Practicing meditation or mindfulness to become more aware of your inner state
- Journaling to explore the interplay of thoughts and emotions in your experiences
- Engaging in activities that integrate mind and body, such as tai chi or qigong
- Before making important decisions, taking time to center yourself and listen to your inner wisdom
- Practicing active listening in conversations, attending to both the intellectual content and the emotional undercurrents
- Regularly checking in with your inner state throughout the day, noticing when you feel aligned or out of balance
- Exploring practices like yoga or body scan meditation to cultivate greater mind-body awareness

Reflection Questions:

1. Recall a time when you felt your thoughts, emotions, and actions were in perfect harmony. What was that experience like?

2. In what situations do you find it most challenging to maintain a clear and tranquil Xin? What

might be clouding your inner heart-mind in these moments?

3. How might your life change if you made decisions consistently from a place of integrated heart-mind wisdom rather than from purely intellectual analysis or emotional impulse?

4. Reflect on a recent conflict or misunderstanding. How might approaching it with an awareness of Xin (both your own and others') have changed the interaction?

5. What practices or activities help you feel most connected to your inner heart-mind? How could you incorporate these more fully into your daily life?

Remember, cultivating Xin is not about achieving a perfect state of inner harmony, but about continually returning to and nurturing our deepest center. It's a lifelong practice of integration, awareness, and alignment with our true nature and the Tao. As you explore this concept, be patient and compassionate with yourself, recognizing that the journey of harmonizing the heart-mind is itself an expression of the Tao.

Chapter 13: Being with Xing (Independent Mind)

Free from chains of rigid thought,
    Xing, the mind that can't be bought,
    Unbound by doctrine, dogma's sway,
    It charts its own authentic way.
    Not rebellious, nor confined,
    But clear and present, unaligned,
    The sage, with Xing as trusted guide,
    In wisdom's boundless realm resides.

Explanation:

Xing (◈) is a complex concept in Chinese philosophy, including Taoism, that can be translated as "nature," "essence," or "independent mind." In Taoist thought, Xing refers to our innate, authentic nature - the part of us that exists prior to societal conditioning and cultural imprinting. It's closely related to the idea of our original self, aligned with the Tao.

The character ◈ (Xing) is composed of two parts: ◈ (xin, heart-mind) and ◈ (sheng, life or birth). This composition suggests that Xing is the innate, living quality of our heart-mind, our essential nature as it emerges into being.

In Taoist philosophy, cultivating and expressing Xing is crucial for living in harmony with the Tao. It involves peeling away layers of acquired habits, beliefs, and social conventions to reveal and act from our true nature. This doesn't mean rejecting all social norms or living in a state of constant rebellion, but rather developing the clarity and courage to discern and follow our authentic path.

The concept of Xing challenges us to question our conditioned responses and societal expectations. It encourages us to think independently, to see things as they are rather than as we've been told they should be. This independent mind is not driven by ego or desire for uniqueness, but by a deep alignment with our inherent nature and the principles of the Tao.

Zhuangzi, one of the foundational Taoist philosophers, often emphasized the importance of Xing. He used colorful stories and parables to illustrate how conventional thinking limits our perspective and separates us from our true nature. For Zhuangzi, cultivating Xing involved a kind of "forgetting" - letting go of fixed ideas and categories to experience reality more directly and spontaneously.

It's important to note that in Taoist thought, Xing is not seen as something separate from the Tao. Our true nature is understood as an expression of the Tao itself. Therefore, by cultivating and expressing our Xing, we naturally come into greater harmony with the fundamental nature of the universe.

Modern Application:

The concept of Xing offers valuable insights for our modern lives:

1. Critical Thinking: Cultivating Xing encourages us to question assumptions and think for ourselves, crucial skills in an age of information overload and misinformation.

2. Authenticity: Understanding Xing can help us live more authentically, making choices aligned with our true nature rather than external expectations.

3. Creativity: By freeing ourselves from conventional thinking, we can access more original and innovative ideas.

4. Personal Growth: Exploring our Xing can lead to profound self-discovery and personal development.

5. Decision Making: An independent mind guided by Xing can help us make decisions that are truly right for us, rather than simply following trends or others' advice.

6. Resilience: A strong sense of our innate nature can provide stability and resilience in the face of external pressures and changes.

7. Leadership: Leaders who operate from their Xing can bring fresh perspectives and authentic vision to their roles.

8. Cultural Understanding: Recognizing the influence of cultural conditioning on our thinking can lead to greater openness and understanding in multicultural contexts.

Practical steps might include:

- Practicing mindfulness to become more aware of your habitual thought patterns and reactions
- Regularly questioning your assumptions and beliefs, asking "Is this really true for me?"
- Engaging in free-writing or stream-of-consciousness exercises to bypass your internal censor and access more authentic thoughts
- Exploring new experiences and perspectives to challenge your existing worldview
- Practicing saying "no" to requests or invitations that don't align with your authentic self
- Spending time in nature or in meditation to quiet external influences and connect with your innate nature
- Engaging in creative activities without concern for the outcome, allowing your authentic expression to emerge

Reflection Questions:

1. Recall a time when you made a decision that went against conventional wisdom but felt deeply

right to you. What guided you in that moment?

2. What beliefs or habits do you hold that might not be truly your own, but inherited from family, culture, or society?

3. In what areas of your life do you feel most authentic and aligned with your true nature? Where do you feel most out of alignment?

4. How might your life change if you consistently made choices based on your Xing rather than external expectations or pressures?

5. What fears or obstacles might be preventing you from more fully expressing your authentic nature?

Remember, cultivating Xing is not about rejecting all external influences or living in isolation from society. Rather, it's about developing the discernment to recognize what truly resonates with our innate nature and the courage to live from that place of authenticity. As you explore this concept, be patient with yourself and remember that aligning with our true nature is a lifelong journey of discovery and refinement.

Chapter 14: Being Wu Xing (Beyond Form)

Beyond the bounds of shape and name,
>   Wu Xing transcends the mortal game,
>   Formless essence, pure and free,
>   The Tao's eternal mystery.
>   Not this, not that, yet all in one,
>   Where limitations are undone,
>   The sage, embracing formlessness,
>   Finds freedom in life's fluid dance.

Explanation:

Wu Xing (◇◇) in Taoist philosophy refers to the state of being "without form" or "formless." This concept is fundamental to understanding the nature of the Tao itself, which is often described as formless, indefinable, and beyond the reach of ordinary perception and conceptualization.

The term Wu Xing combines two characters: ◇ (Wu), meaning "not have" or "without," and ◇ (Xing), meaning "form" or "shape." Together, they point to a reality that transcends the limitations of physical form and conceptual definition.

In the Tao Te Ching, Lao Tzu frequently alludes to this formless nature of the Tao:

"The Tao that can be told is not the eternal Tao.

The name that can be named is not the eternal name.

The nameless is the beginning of heaven and earth.

The named is the mother of ten thousand things."

This passage highlights the paradox of Wu Xing - that the ultimate reality is beyond form and name, yet it gives rise to all forms and names. It's the formless source from which all manifested reality emerges.

Understanding Wu Xing involves a shift in perception and consciousness. It invites us to look beyond the surface appearances of things to recognize the underlying, formless essence. This doesn't mean denying or rejecting the world of form, but rather seeing it as a temporary manifestation of something more fundamental and unchanging.

For the Taoist sage, cultivating an awareness of Wu Xing leads to a profound sense of freedom and flexibility. By not being bound to fixed forms or rigid definitions, one can adapt fluidly to changing circumstances and see beyond apparent limitations.

Wu Xing is also closely related to the Taoist practices of "fasting of the mind" and "sitting in forgetfulness," where one aims to release all fixed notions and preconceptions to experience reality more directly and authentically.

Modern Application:

The concept of Wu Xing offers valuable insights for our modern lives:

1. Adaptability: Embracing formlessness can enhance our ability to adapt to rapidly changing circumstances in our personal and professional lives.

2. Creativity: Understanding Wu Xing can free us from creative blocks by helping us see beyond conventional forms and categories.

3. Problem-solving: Approaching problems from a formless perspective can lead to innovative solutions that aren't constrained by traditional thinking.

4. Personal Growth: Recognizing our own formless nature can liberate us from limiting self-concepts and open up new possibilities for growth and transformation.

5. Stress Reduction: Cultivating an awareness of the formless can provide a sense of spaciousness and freedom in the face of life's challenges.

6. Relationships: Seeing beyond fixed roles and expectations in relationships can lead to more authentic and fluid connections.

7. Spiritual Practice: Many forms of meditation and contemplative practice aim to cultivate an awareness of formless reality.

8. Leadership: Leaders who understand Wu Xing can create more flexible and responsive organizations, able to adapt to changing environments.

Practical steps might include:

- Practicing formless meditation, focusing on the space of awareness rather than on specific objects or thoughts
- Engaging in creative exercises that challenge conventional forms, such as abstract art or experimental music
- Regularly questioning your assumptions about the fixed nature of things in your life
- Spending time in nature, observing how forms constantly change and transform
- Experimenting with taking on different roles or perspectives to loosen your attachment to a fixed identity
- Practicing seeing the spaces between things, the background as well as the foreground
- When faced with a problem, try approaching it as if you had no preconceived notions about what the solution should look like

Reflection Questions:

1. Can you recall a moment when you experienced a sense of formlessness or boundlessness? How

did this experience affect your perception of reality?

2. In what areas of your life do you feel most bound by fixed forms or definitions? How might embracing Wu Xing change your approach to these areas?

3. How does the idea that your true nature is formless challenge or support your current self-concept?

4. Reflect on a current challenge in your life. How might viewing it from a formless perspective open up new possibilities or solutions?

5. How could embracing Wu Xing change your relationship to change and uncertainty in your life?

Remember, the concept of Wu Xing is not about escaping or denying the world of form, but about recognizing the deeper, formless reality that underlies and gives rise to all forms. As you explore this concept, allow yourself to rest in the spaciousness of not-knowing, embracing the mystery and potential that exists beyond the boundaries of defined forms and fixed ideas.

Chapter 15: Being an Unhurried Daoist

In a world of haste and hurry's strife,
>   The sage moves at the pace of life,
>   Unhurried, calm, in Tao's embrace,
>   Each moment lived with subtle grace.
>   Not lazy, slack, or left behind,
>   But present, whole in heart and mind,
>   In nature's rhythm, gently flows,
>   The way of Tao, the sage well knows.

Explanation:

The concept of being an "unhurried Daoist" is not explicitly named in classical Taoist texts, but it embodies a core principle of Taoist philosophy - the idea of moving in harmony with the natural flow of the Tao, without forcing or rushing.

In the Tao Te Ching, Lao Tzu often uses images of nature to illustrate this unhurried way of being. Water, for instance, is frequently cited as an example of strength through softness and effectiveness through non-contention. Water doesn't rush to its destination but flows naturally, following the path of least resistance, yet over time it can carve canyons and shape landscapes.

This unhurried approach is closely related to the Taoist concept of wu wei, or "non-action." Wu wei doesn't mean doing nothing, but rather acting in a way that's in harmony with the natural order of things. It's about finding the right moment to act and then doing so with minimal effort.

The unhurried Daoist understands that everything has its own natural timing. Just as we can't force a flower to bloom before its time, we can't force the natural unfolding of events in our lives. Instead, we learn to attune ourselves to the rhythms of nature and the Tao.

This doesn't mean being passive or lazy. The unhurried Daoist is still active and engaged with life, but from a place of inner calm and alignment with the Tao. There's a recognition that often, slowing down actually allows us to accomplish more, as we act more efficiently and with greater awareness.

In the Zhuangzi, another key Taoist text, there are many stories that illustrate this unhurried approach to life. These often feature sages or skilled artisans who achieve remarkable results not through frantic effort, but through a deep, unhurried attunement to their task and environment.

Modern Application:

The principle of being an unhurried Daoist offers valuable insights for our fast-paced modern lives:

1. Stress Reduction: Adopting an unhurried approach can significantly reduce stress and anxiety, allowing for a more peaceful and enjoyable life.

2. Productivity: Counterintuitively, slowing down can often lead to greater productivity as we work more efficiently and make fewer mistakes.

3. Decision Making: An unhurried approach allows for more thoughtful and balanced decision-making, rather than reactive choices.

4. Relationships: Being present and unhurried in our interactions can lead to deeper, more meaningful connections with others.

5. Creativity: Many creative insights come when we slow down and allow our minds to wander, rather than constantly pushing for results.

6. Health: Chronic rushing and stress can have negative health impacts. An unhurried lifestyle can contribute to better physical and mental health.

7. Appreciation: Moving more slowly through life allows us to notice and appreciate details we might otherwise miss.

8. Sustainability: An unhurried approach often aligns with more sustainable lifestyle choices, as we're less likely to engage in wasteful consumption.

Practical steps might include:

- Practicing mindfulness or meditation to cultivate a sense of presence and calm
- Building buffer time into your schedule to avoid constant rushing
- Eating meals slowly and mindfully, savoring each bite
- Taking regular breaks during work to reset and refocus
- Engaging in activities like tai chi, qigong, or yoga that encourage slow, mindful movement
- Spending time in nature, observing its unhurried rhythms
- Practicing "monotasking" instead of multitasking, giving full attention to one thing at a time
- Setting aside time for unstructured relaxation or play

Reflection Questions:

1. Reflect on a recent experience where you felt rushed or hurried. How did it affect your state of mind and the quality of your actions?

2. Can you recall a time when slowing down actually helped you accomplish something more effectively? What did you learn from this experience?

3. What areas of your life might benefit most from adopting a more unhurried approach? What would this look like in practice?

4. How does the idea of being "unhurried" challenge or support your current values and goals?

5. What fears or beliefs might be driving you to rush unnecessarily in your daily life?

Remember, becoming an unhurried Daoist is not about suddenly changing your entire lifestyle, but about gradually cultivating a different relationship with time and action. It's a practice of continually returning to the present moment and aligning with the natural flow of life. As you explore this approach, be patient with yourself and notice the subtle shifts in your experience as you learn to move through life with greater ease and harmony.

Chapter 16: Being with Heng (Constancy)

In the flux of life's swift stream,

    Heng stands firm, a constant beam,

    Not rigid, fixed, or set in stone,

    But true to Tao, and that alone.

    Through change and chaos, calm resides,

    In Heng, the sage securely glides,

    Embracing flow, yet anchored deep,

    This balance, wise ones always keep.

Explanation:

Heng (◈) is a concept in Taoist philosophy that can be translated as "constancy," "permanence," or "duration." However, it's important to understand that this constancy is not about rigidity or unchanging fixedness. Rather, Heng refers to a kind of underlying continuity or enduring principle that persists through all changes. In the Tao Te Ching, Lao Tzu speaks of the importance of aligning oneself with the constant Tao:

"He who knows the constant is called enlightened.

He who does not know the constant is the source of disorder."

This constancy is not opposed to change but is rather what allows change to occur. It's the unchanging background against which all changes take place, or the thread that runs through all transformations.

The concept of Heng is closely related to the idea of the Tao itself, which is described as eternal and unchanging, yet gives rise to all the changes in the world. By cultivating Heng, we connect with this underlying constancy and find stability amidst the flux of life.

In Taoist practice, Heng is often associated with steadfastness in cultivation and meditation. It's about maintaining a consistent practice and a steady mind, regardless of external circumstances. This doesn't mean being inflexible, but rather having a stable center from which to respond fluidly to life's changes.

Heng also relates to the natural cycles and rhythms of the universe. The constancy of these cycles - day and night, the seasons, the phases of the moon - provides a framework within which all changes occur. By attuning ourselves to these natural rhythms, we can find our own sense of constancy.

Modern Application:

The principle of Heng offers valuable insights for navigating our often turbulent modern lives:

1. Resilience: Cultivating inner constancy can help us remain stable and centered in the face of external changes and challenges.

2. Habit Formation: Understanding Heng can support the development of positive, consistent habits in our personal and professional lives.

3. Relationships: Constancy in our core values and commitments can foster trust and depth in our relationships.

4. Career Development: Long-term career success often depends on consistent effort and dedication, aligned with the principle of Heng.

5. Mental Health: A sense of inner constancy can provide an anchor during times of emotional turbulence or stress.

6. Leadership: Leaders who embody Heng can provide stable guidance and inspire trust, even in uncertain times.

7. Personal Growth: Consistent practice and effort, guided by Heng, are key to long-term personal development and spiritual growth.

8. Environmental Stewardship: Recognizing the constancy of natural cycles can inspire more sustainable, long-term thinking about our relationship with the environment.

Practical steps might include:

- Establishing a regular meditation or mindfulness practice to cultivate inner stability
- Creating and sticking to supportive daily routines
- Regularly reflecting on and reaffirming your core values
- Practicing patience and perseverance in pursuing long-term goals
- Observing natural cycles in your environment and aligning your activities with them when possible
- In times of change or stress, focusing on what remains constant in your life
- Cultivating relationships and commitments that you can maintain over the long term
- Regularly reviewing and recommitting to your personal or professional mission

Reflection Questions:

1. What elements in your life provide a sense of constancy or stability? How do these anchor you during times of change?

2. Reflect on a time when you maintained consistency in the face of challenges. What internal resources did you draw upon?

3. In what areas of your life do you struggle to maintain constancy? What might be the root causes of this inconsistency?

4. How might embracing the principle of Heng change your approach to your goals and

aspirations?

5. Consider the natural cycles in your environment (daily, seasonal, etc.). How might aligning more closely with these cycles bring more constancy to your life?

Remember, cultivating Heng is not about becoming rigid or resistant to change. It's about finding an inner stability that allows you to flow with life's changes while remaining true to your essential nature and values. As you explore this concept, notice how moments of constancy arise naturally when you're aligned with the Tao, and how this inner stability can become a source of strength and peace in your life.

Chapter 17: Being as a Sage

Neither saint nor common soul,

    The sage embodies Tao's whole,

    In simplicity, profound,

    In action, stillness can be found.

    Embracing all, yet holding none,

    Through wisdom, not by rule, it's done.

    The sage, a mirror of the Way,

    In being, not in words, holds sway.

Explanation:

The concept of the sage (◇◇, shèngrén) is central to Taoist philosophy. The sage represents the ideal of a person who has fully realized the Tao and embodies its principles in their being and actions. However, it's crucial to understand that the Taoist sage is not a distant, otherworldly figure, but rather a model of how we can live in harmony with the natural order of the universe. In the Tao Te Ching, Lao Tzu frequently describes the qualities and actions of the sage:

"The sage does not hoard.

The more he helps others, the more he benefits himself,

The more he gives to others, the more he gets himself.

The Way of Heaven does one good but never does one harm.

The Way of the sage is to act but not to compete."

These passages highlight key aspects of the sage's character: selflessness, non-attachment, alignment with natural principles, and action without force or competition.

The sage in Taoist thought is often described paradoxically. They are said to know everything yet claim to know nothing, to act without acting, to lead without dominating. This reflects the sage's transcendence of ordinary dualities and their alignment with the paradoxical nature of the Tao itself.

Importantly, the sage is not someone who has withdrawn from the world, but someone who engages with it fully, yet without being caught up in its conflicts and desires. They respond to situations with spontaneous wisdom, not bound by rigid rules or doctrines.

The sage embodies wu wei, acting in harmony with the natural flow of things rather than forcing their will upon the world. They are like water, taking the shape of any container yet always flowing to the lowest place, symbolizing humility and adaptability.

Modern Application:

The ideal of the Taoist sage offers valuable insights for our modern lives:

1. Leadership: The sage's model of leading without dominating can inspire more collaborative and effective leadership styles.

2. Decision Making: The sage's ability to respond spontaneously to situations can guide us in making more intuitive and contextually appropriate decisions.

3. Stress Management: The sage's inner peace and non-attachment can inspire practices for managing stress and maintaining equilibrium in challenging times.

4. Relationships: The sage's selflessness and ability to embrace all without possession can guide us in fostering healthier, more compassionate relationships.

5. Personal Growth: The journey of becoming sage-like is a powerful model for ongoing personal development and self-cultivation.

6. Conflict Resolution: The sage's ability to transcend dualities can inspire more holistic approaches to resolving conflicts.

7. Environmental Stewardship: The sage's harmony with nature can guide us in developing more sustainable lifestyles and policies.

8. Creativity: The sage's spontaneity and alignment with the Tao can inspire more authentic and flowing creative expression.

Practical steps might include:

- Practicing mindfulness to cultivate present-moment awareness and spontaneous responsiveness
- Regularly reflecting on your motivations to cultivate greater selflessness
- Studying nature to learn from its effortless efficiency and apply these principles in your life
- Practicing letting go of attachments, both material and psychological
- Cultivating humility by regularly acknowledging what you don't know
- Engaging in activities that challenge your usual ways of thinking and acting
- Seeking opportunities to serve others without expectation of reward
- Practicing wu wei by identifying areas where you might be using unnecessary force and finding more harmonious approaches

Reflection Questions:

1. Reflect on a person in your life who embodies sage-like qualities. What specific traits or actions make them seem wise to you?

2. In what areas of your life do you find it most challenging to embody sage-like qualities? What obstacles do you face?

3. How might your life and relationships change if you consistently acted from a place of

selflessness and non-attachment?

4. Consider a recent conflict or challenge. How might a sage-like perspective have changed your approach to the situation?

5. What aspects of the sage's way of being do you find most inspiring or challenging? Why?

Remember, the ideal of the sage is not about achieving perfection or becoming superhuman. It's about gradually aligning ourselves more closely with the Tao, cultivating wisdom through our daily lives and interactions. As you contemplate these ideas, consider how you might bring more sage-like qualities into your everyday experiences, always with patience and compassion for yourself and others.

Chapter 18: Being Without Fa (Rules)

Beyond the bounds of should and must,

    In Tao's flow, we learn to trust,

    Not lawless, wild, or unrestrained,

    But by inner wisdom sustained.

    Fa's rigid forms we gently shed,

    By nature's subtle ways instead,

    The sage, in freedom's dance sublime,

    Moves with the Tao's perfect rhyme.

Explanation:

The concept of being without Fa (◇, fǎ), or rules, is a nuanced and often misunderstood aspect of Taoist philosophy. It doesn't advocate for a complete absence of structure or a descent into chaos, but rather points to a way of being that transcends rigid, externally imposed rules in favor of spontaneous alignment with the Tao.

In traditional Chinese thought, Fa refers to human-made laws, methods, or standards. While these have their place in organizing society, Taoism recognizes that such rigid structures can often conflict with the natural flow of the Tao and the inherent wisdom of our true nature.

Lao Tzu, in the Tao Te Ching, often critiques the proliferation of laws and rules:

"The more laws and restrictions there are,

The poorer people become.

...

The more rules and regulations,

The more thieves and robbers."

This passage suggests that an overreliance on external rules can actually create more problems than it solves, as it disconnects people from their innate sense of harmony and balance.

Instead of rigid rules, Taoism emphasizes cultivating De (virtue or power) that arises naturally from one's alignment with the Tao. This inner virtue guides one's actions more effectively and harmoniously than any set of external rules could.

However, it's crucial to understand that being without Fa doesn't mean acting recklessly or selfishly. Instead, it means developing the wisdom to respond appropriately to each unique situation, guided by one's understanding of the Tao rather than by fixed precepts.

This approach aligns closely with the Taoist concept of wu wei, or non-action. When we're not bound by rigid rules, we can act more spontaneously and effectively, in harmony with the natural flow of circumstances.

Modern Application:

The principle of being without Fa offers valuable insights for our rule-laden modern lives:

1. Creativity: Letting go of rigid rules can unlock greater creativity and innovation in various fields.

2. Problem-solving: A more flexible approach can lead to novel solutions that might be overlooked when strictly following established methods.

3. Personal Growth: Moving beyond rigid self-imposed rules can lead to more authentic self-expression and development.

4. Leadership: Leaders who can balance structure with flexibility often create more adaptable and resilient organizations.

5. Education: Learning to think beyond rules and formulas can lead to deeper understanding and more effective application of knowledge.

6. Ethics: Developing inner virtue can lead to more nuanced and contextually appropriate ethical decisions than simply following rigid moral codes.

7. Relationships: Moving beyond prescribed roles and expectations can lead to more genuine and fulfilling connections.

8. Stress Reduction: Letting go of the need to always follow rules perfectly can reduce anxiety and increase overall well-being.

Practical steps might include:

- Practicing mindfulness to become more aware of habitual patterns and reactions
- Regularly questioning the rules and assumptions you operate under, asking if they truly serve the situation
- Engaging in free-form creative activities without predetermined structures or outcomes
- In decision-making, considering the unique context of each situation rather than always defaulting to standard procedures
- Practicing spontaneity in safe, low-stakes situations to become more comfortable with unstructured responses
- Studying nature to observe how natural systems function harmoniously without imposed rules
- Exploring improvisational arts (music, dance, theater) to cultivate spontaneous responsiveness
- Reflecting on times when breaking a rule led to a positive outcome, and what guided your actions in those moments

Reflection Questions:

1. What self-imposed rules or expectations might be limiting your growth or happiness? How might letting go of these change your life?

2. Can you recall a situation where following a rule led to a suboptimal outcome? How might a more flexible approach have changed things?

3. In what areas of your life do you feel most constrained by rules or conventions? How might you bring more spontaneity and natural responsiveness to these areas?

4. How does the idea of being guided by inner virtue rather than external rules challenge or support your current worldview?

5. What fears or concerns arise when you consider letting go of certain rules in your life? What might these reveal about your beliefs and attachments?

Remember, being without Fa is not about rejecting all structure or living in a state of constant unpredictability. It's about developing the wisdom to know when to adhere to structure and when to flow more freely, always guided by your alignment with the Tao. As you explore this concept, be patient with yourself and notice how moments of spontaneous wisdom naturally arise when you're not bound by rigid rules.

Chapter 19: Being Without Ai (Attachment)

Free from clinging's binding chains,
    The sage in boundless freedom reigns,
    Not cold or distant, but aware,
    Embracing all with equal care.
    Ai's grip released, the heart expands,
    In letting go, true love withstands,
    The Tao flows free through open hands,
    As wisdom's light across all lands.

Explanation:

The concept of being without Ai (愛, ài), or attachment, is a profound and often misunderstood aspect of Taoist philosophy. In this context, Ai doesn't refer to love in its purest form, but rather to the clinging, possessive aspect of what we often call love. The Taoist ideal is to love without attachment, to care deeply without the need to possess or control. In the Tao Te Ching, Lao Tzu alludes to this idea in various ways:

"The Master gives himself up

to whatever the moment brings.

He knows that he is going to die,

and he has nothing left to hold on to:

no illusions in his mind,

no resistances in his body."

This passage illustrates the freedom that comes from releasing attachments, even to life itself. It's not about becoming indifferent, but about developing a deep acceptance of the impermanent nature of all things. The Taoist sage cultivates a state of non-attachment that allows them to engage fully with life without being bound by desires or fears. This doesn't mean they don't care or don't have relationships, but that they relate to the world with an open hand rather than a closed fist.

Non-attachment in Taoism is closely related to the concept of wu wei, or non-doing. When we're not attached to specific outcomes, we can act more spontaneously and effectively, in harmony with the natural flow of the Tao. It's important to note that being without attachment doesn't mean living a life devoid of love or connection. On the contrary, it allows for a more expansive, unconditional form of love that isn't limited by personal desires or expectations.

Modern Application:

The principle of being without Ai offers valuable insights for our often attachment-driven modern lives:

1. Relationships: Practicing non-attachment can lead to healthier, more genuine relationships where we appreciate others without trying to possess or control them.

2. Stress Reduction: Letting go of attachments to specific outcomes can significantly reduce anxiety and stress in various life situations.

3. Adaptability: Being less attached to our ideas, possessions, or status can make us more adaptable to change.

4. Decision Making: Non-attachment can lead to clearer, more objective decision-making, unbiased by personal desires or fears.

5. Creativity: Letting go of attachment to particular ideas or methods can open up new realms of creative possibility.

6. Personal Growth: Releasing attachments to our self-image or past experiences can allow for

more authentic personal development.

7. Mindfulness: The practice of non-attachment is closely linked to mindfulness, helping us stay present and aware.

8. Grief and Loss: Understanding and practicing non-attachment can help us navigate loss and change with greater resilience and peace.

Practical steps might include:

- Practicing mindfulness meditation to observe thoughts and feelings without clinging to them
- Regularly reflecting on the impermanent nature of all things
- Practicing generosity and letting go of material possessions
- In relationships, focusing on appreciating the present moment rather than expecting or demanding particular outcomes
- When working towards goals, focusing on the process rather than being overly attached to the result
- Practicing acceptance of situations as they are, before deciding if action is needed
- Exploring minimalism or simplicity in lifestyle to reduce attachments to material things
- When experiencing strong emotions, practice observing them without immediately reacting

Reflection Questions:

1. What are you most attached to in your life right now? How does this attachment affect your thoughts, emotions, and actions?

2. Can you recall a time when letting go of an attachment led to an unexpected positive outcome? What did this experience teach you?

3. How might your relationships change if you practiced loving without attachment?

4. In what areas of your life do you struggle most with letting go? What fears or beliefs might be underlying these attachments?

5. How does the idea of non-attachment challenge or support your current understanding of love and care?

Remember, cultivating non-attachment is a gradual process. It's not about forcing yourself to not care, but about developing a wider, more accepting perspective. As you explore this concept, be patient with yourself and notice how moments of non-attachment can bring a sense of freedom and peace. The goal is not to eliminate all attachments overnight, but to gradually loosen their hold, allowing for a more flowing, harmonious way of being.

Chapter 20: Being Without Zhi (Striving)

In the dance of life's ebb and flow,
        The sage learns to let striving go,
        Not idle, lazy, or inert,
        But in Tao's current, free from hurt.
        Zhi's anxious push we gently ease,
        As natural action brings us peace,
        In wu wei's grace, we find our way,
        As effortless as night to day.

Explanation:

The concept of being without Zhi (志, zhì), or striving, is a fundamental principle in Taoist philosophy. Zhi typically refers to ambition, will, or determination. While these qualities are often praised in many cultures, Taoism recognizes that excessive striving can lead to tension, anxiety, and a disconnection from the natural flow of the Tao.

In the Tao Te Ching, Lao Tzu frequently advises against forceful striving:

"Do you want to improve the world?

I don't think it can be done.

The world is sacred.

It can't be improved.

If you tamper with it, you'll ruin it.

If you treat it like an object, you'll lose it."

This passage illustrates the Taoist view that trying too hard to control or improve things often leads to unintended negative consequences. Instead, the sage learns to work with the natural tendencies of people and situations, rather than against them.

Being without Zhi doesn't mean becoming passive or apathetic. Rather, it's about aligning our actions with the natural flow of the Tao, acting without force or excessive effort. This principle is closely related to the concept of wu wei, or "non-doing," which advocates for action that arises spontaneously from our alignment with the Tao.

The Taoist sage understands that the universe has its own rhythm and order. By letting go of the need to constantly strive and control, we can tap into this natural order and act more effectively and harmoniously.

Modern Application:

The principle of being without Zhi offers valuable insights for our often ambition-driven modern lives:

1. Stress Reduction: Letting go of constant striving can significantly reduce stress and anxiety, leading to better mental and physical health.

2. Efficiency: Paradoxically, letting go of forceful effort often leads to more efficient and effective action.

3. Creativity: Releasing the pressure to strive can open up space for more natural, spontaneous creativity.

4. Relationships: Approaching relationships without agenda or forceful expectations can lead to more genuine and harmonious connections.

5. Career Development: Understanding when to push and when to flow can lead to more sustainable and fulfilling career progression.

6. Problem Solving: Sometimes, letting go of striving allows solutions to emerge naturally that we might have overlooked through forceful effort.

7. Personal Growth: Embracing this principle can lead to a more balanced, self-accepting approach to personal development.

8. Environmental Awareness: Recognizing the wisdom in natural systems can inspire more harmonious, less forceful approaches to environmental issues.

Practical steps might include:

- Practicing mindfulness to become more aware of when you're striving unnecessarily
- Incorporating regular periods of "non-doing" into your day, where you simply be without trying to accomplish anything
- When faced with a challenge, pause to consider whether forceful action is truly necessary
- Observing nature to learn from its effortless efficiency
- Practicing acceptance of current situations before deciding if action is needed
- Exploring activities that encourage flow states, where action becomes effortless
- In your work, focus on aligning with the natural rhythm of your energy and creativity rather than forcing productivity
- When making decisions, try waiting for the right moment to act rather than pushing for immediate results

Reflection Questions:

1. In what areas of your life do you find yourself striving the most? What drives this striving?

2. Can you recall a time when letting go of striving led to a better outcome? What did this experience teach you?

3. How might your life change if you approached your goals with less forceful striving and more alignment with natural rhythms?

4. What fears or beliefs might be driving your need to strive or control outcomes?

5. How does the idea of acting without striving challenge or support your current understanding of success and achievement?

Remember, being without Zhi is not about giving up on goals or becoming inactive. It's about finding a more harmonious, less forceful way of engaging with life and achieving what needs to be done. As you explore this concept, pay attention to moments when things flow naturally without excessive effort. These can be opportunities to learn about your own alignment with the Tao and to cultivate a more effortless way of being in the world.

Chapter 21: Being the Daoist Paradox

In contrast's dance, truth comes to light,

    The weak is strong, the dark is bright,

    Paradox, the Dao's sweet song,

    Where right meets wrong, and short meets long.

    The sage embraces opposite's play,

    Finding balance in disarray,

    For in life's vast perplexity,

    Lies wisdom's deepest mystery.

Explanation:

The Daoist paradox is a central theme in Taoist philosophy, embodying the recognition that apparent opposites are often interconnected, interdependent, and even complementary. This concept challenges our usual either/or thinking, inviting us to embrace a both/and perspective that sees the unity underlying apparent duality.

In the Tao Te Ching, Lao Tzu frequently uses paradoxical statements to convey deep truths:

"The Tao that can be told is not the eternal Tao.

The name that can be named is not the eternal name."

"When people see some things as beautiful,

other things become ugly.

When people see some things as good,

other things become bad."

These passages illustrate how our judgments and categorizations often create artificial divisions in what is essentially a unified whole. The Daoist paradox encourages us to look beyond these surface-level distinctions to perceive the underlying unity of all things.

The concept of yin and yang is perhaps the most well-known expression of the Daoist paradox. This symbol represents how seemingly opposite forces are actually interconnected and interdependent. Light cannot exist without darkness, strength is defined by weakness, and so on.

The Daoist sage understands that life is full of paradoxes and embraces them rather than trying to resolve them into a single, consistent viewpoint. This approach allows for a more flexible, nuanced understanding of reality that can adapt to the ever-changing nature of existence.

Modern Application:

Understanding and embracing the Daoist paradox can offer valuable insights for navigating our complex modern lives:

1. Problem Solving: Recognizing the interconnectedness of apparent opposites can lead to more holistic, creative solutions to complex problems.

2. Conflict Resolution: Seeing beyond either/or positions can help in finding compromises and mutual understanding in conflicts.

3. Personal Growth: Embracing our own internal contradictions can lead to greater self-acceptance and more authentic personal development.

4. Decision Making: Understanding paradox can help in making more balanced decisions that consider multiple perspectives.

5. Stress Management: Accepting life's paradoxes can reduce anxiety caused by trying to force everything into consistent, non-contradictory categories.

6. Creativity: Paradoxical thinking can spark creativity by encouraging novel associations and ideas.

7. Leadership: Leaders who understand paradox can navigate complex situations more effectively, balancing competing needs and perspectives.

8. Environmental Awareness: Recognizing the paradoxical nature of ecosystems can lead to more nuanced, effective approaches to environmental issues.

Practical steps might include:

- Practicing mindfulness to observe the coexistence of seemingly contradictory thoughts or feelings
- When faced with a binary choice, try to find a "third way" that incorporates elements of both options
- In conflicts, look for the valid points on both sides rather than assuming one side must be entirely right
- Explore practices like Zen koans that use paradox to challenge habitual thinking
- In personal development, work on cultivating apparently opposite qualities (e.g., strength and flexibility, confidence and humility)
- When problem-solving, deliberately consider perspectives that seem to contradict your initial approach
- In creative work, experiment with combining seemingly incompatible elements or ideas
- Practice holding space for uncertainty and ambiguity rather than always seeking clear-cut answers

Reflection Questions:

1. Can you think of a situation in your life that embodies a paradox? How might embracing both sides of this paradox change your perspective?

2. How do you typically respond to contradictions or inconsistencies? How might a more paradoxical approach change your reactions?

3. In what areas of your life do you tend to think in either/or terms? How might a both/and perspective shift your approach?

4. Reflect on a recent conflict or disagreement. Can you see how both sides might be simultaneously true in some way?

5. How does the idea of embracing paradox challenge or support your current worldview and beliefs?

Remember, embracing the Daoist paradox isn't about logically resolving all contradictions, but about becoming comfortable with the inherent complexities and apparent contradictions of existence. As you explore this concept, notice how accepting paradox can lead to a more flexible, nuanced understanding of yourself and the world around you. The goal is not to eliminate all sense of distinction, but to recognize the underlying unity that connects apparent opposites.

Chapter 22: Being with Rou (Flexibility)

Like willows bending in the breeze,
>The sage flows with life's mysteries,
>Rou's supple strength, both firm and light,
>Yields to darkness, bends toward light.
>Not weak or frail, but deeply strong,
>Adapting as we move along,
>In flexibility we find,
>The Tao's own resilient mind.

Explanation:

Rou (◇), often translated as "softness" or "flexibility," is a key concept in Taoist philosophy. It represents a quality of yielding and adaptability that, paradoxically, is seen as a source of great strength and resilience. This principle is often illustrated through natural metaphors, such as water that can wear away stone or a young sapling that bends in the wind while a rigid old tree breaks.

In the Tao Te Ching, Lao Tzu frequently extols the virtues of softness and flexibility:

"Nothing in the world
is as soft and yielding as water.
Yet for dissolving the hard and inflexible,
nothing can surpass it."
"The soft overcomes the hard;
the gentle overcomes the rigid."

These passages highlight the Taoist understanding that true strength lies not in rigid resistance, but in the ability to adapt and flow with circumstances. The sage who embodies Rou doesn't fight against the natural course of events but learns to move with them, maintaining inner balance and effectiveness.

Importantly, Rou is not about being weak or passive. Rather, it's about cultivating a kind of strength that comes from alignment with the Tao – a strength that is responsive, adaptable, and ultimately more enduring than rigid force.

The concept of Rou is closely related to the principle of wu wei, or "non-action." By remaining flexible and yielding, we can often achieve our aims more effectively than through forceful action, allowing situations to resolve themselves naturally.

Modern Application:

The principle of Rou offers valuable insights for navigating our often rigid and fast-paced modern lives:

1. Stress Management: Cultivating flexibility in our thoughts and reactions can significantly reduce stress and increase resilience in the face of challenges.

2. Conflict Resolution: A flexible approach can help in finding creative solutions to conflicts, allowing for compromise and mutual understanding.

3. Career Development: In a rapidly changing job market, the ability to adapt and learn new skills (embodying Rou) is increasingly valuable.

4. Relationships: Flexibility in our expectations and behaviors can lead to more harmonious and lasting relationships.

5. Problem Solving: A flexible mindset allows for more creative and effective problem-solving, especially in complex or uncertain situations.

6. Personal Growth: Embracing Rou can help us adapt to life's changes more gracefully and turn challenges into opportunities for growth.

7. Leadership: Leaders who embody flexibility can guide their teams more effectively through changing circumstances.

8. Health and Wellness: The principle of Rou aligns with practices like yoga and tai chi, which cultivate both physical and mental flexibility.

Practical steps might include:

- Practicing physical activities that promote flexibility, such as yoga or tai chi
- When faced with opposition, experiment with yielding or redirecting energy rather than meeting force with force
- In conversations, practice active listening and being open to changing your viewpoint
- Regularly step out of your comfort zone to build adaptability
- When plans change unexpectedly, practice accepting and adapting rather than resisting
- In problem-solving, try approaching the issue from multiple angles rather than insisting on one approach
- Practice mindfulness to become more aware of when you're being rigid in your thoughts or behaviors
- In conflicts, look for areas where you can be flexible without compromising your core values

Reflection Questions:

1. Recall a time when being flexible led to a positive outcome. What did this experience teach you about the strength of yielding?

2. In what areas of your life do you tend to be most rigid? How might cultivating more flexibility

in these areas benefit you?

3. How does the idea of strength through flexibility challenge or support your current understanding of power and effectiveness?

4. Think of someone you know who embodies the quality of Rou. How does their flexibility manifest, and what effect does it have on their life and relationships?

5. How might embracing Rou change your approach to current challenges or goals in your life?

Remember, cultivating Rou is not about becoming a pushover or abandoning all structure. It's about developing a kind of resilient flexibility that allows you to navigate life's challenges with grace and effectiveness. As you explore this concept, pay attention to moments when yielding or adapting feels more powerful than resisting. These can be opportunities to deepen your understanding and practice of Rou in your daily life.

Chapter 23: Being Ziran (Naturally)

In harmony with nature's way,

    Ziran guides us day by day,

    Not forced or feigned, but true and free,

    As flowers bloom, as rivers flee.

    The sage in naturalness abides,

    No pretense wears, no essence hides,

    For in our depths, when masks fall through,

    The Tao reveals what's ever true.

Explanation:

Ziran (◇◇), often translated as "naturalness" or "spontaneity," is a fundamental concept in Taoist philosophy. It refers to the innate, spontaneous way of being that arises when we're in harmony with the Tao. Ziran is about allowing things to be as they are, following their own nature without interference or forced effort. In the Tao Te Ching, Lao Tzu speaks of Ziran as a key attribute of the Tao itself:

"Man follows the earth.

Earth follows the universe.

The universe follows the Tao.

The Tao follows what is natural."

This passage illustrates the Taoist view that the highest wisdom lies in aligning ourselves with the natural order of things, rather than imposing our will upon the world. Ziran doesn't mean passivity or a return to a primitive state. Rather, it suggests that our truest actions and most authentic expressions arise when we're in touch with our essential nature and the nature of the world around us. It's about allowing things to unfold according to their own intrinsic principles, rather than trying to control or manipulate them based on our limited understanding. The concept of Ziran is closely related to wu wei, or "non-action." Both principles encourage a way of being that is in harmony with the Tao, free from forced effort or artificial constraints. However, while wu wei focuses on non-interference, Ziran emphasizes the inherent authenticity and spontaneity of all things.

Modern Application:

The principle of Ziran offers valuable insights for our often over-controlled and artificially structured modern lives:

1. Self-acceptance: Instead of trying to force ourselves to fit an idealized image, we can practice

accepting our natural inclinations and authentic selves.

2. Creativity: By letting go of rigid expectations and allowing ideas to flow naturally, we can tap into a more authentic and spontaneous form of creativity.

3. Decision-making: Trusting our intuition and natural instincts can lead to decisions that are more aligned with our true selves and the reality of situations.

4. Stress reduction: Embracing Ziran can help us let go of the need to control everything, reducing anxiety and stress.

5. Relationships: Allowing ourselves and others to be authentic can lead to more genuine and fulfilling connections.

6. Personal growth: Instead of forcing change, we can focus on removing obstacles to our natural development and allowing growth to occur organically.

7. Leadership: Leaders who embody Ziran can create environments that allow for more authentic expression and natural problem-solving.

8. Environmental stewardship: Understanding and working with natural processes rather than against them can lead to more sustainable practices.

Practical steps might include:

- Practicing mindfulness to become more aware of your natural inclinations and responses
- Engaging in free-form creative activities without judgment or expectation
- Spending time in nature, observing how natural systems function effortlessly
- Before making decisions, checking in with your intuition and bodily sensations
- Practicing authenticity in your interactions, letting go of the need to present a particular image
- Identifying areas of your life where you're expending unnecessary effort and exploring ways to let go
- Experimenting with unstructured time, allowing yourself to follow your natural rhythms and interests
- In problem-solving, considering what solution feels most natural or effortless

Reflection Questions:
1. When do you feel most natural and authentic in your life? What characterizes these moments?

2. In what areas of your life do you feel you're forcing things or going against your nature? How might embracing Ziran change these situations?

3. How does the idea of following your natural inclinations challenge or support your current goals and aspirations?

4. Think of a time when you allowed something to unfold naturally, without forcing it. What was

the outcome, and how did it feel different from times when you exerted more control?

5. How might your relationships change if you and others felt free to be more natural and spontaneous?

Remember, embracing Ziran doesn't mean abandoning all structure or responsibility. Instead, it's about finding a way of living that feels more effortless and aligned with your true nature and the natural flow of the universe. As you explore this concept, be patient with yourself and allow your understanding to develop naturally over time. The goal is not to force yourself to be natural (which would be a contradiction), but to gradually remove the obstacles that prevent your natural self from shining through.

Chapter 24: Being Without Yu (Excess)

In simplicity's embrace we find,
> The path to peace of heart and mind,
> Without excess, we come to see,
> The essence of true harmony.
> Yu's clutter cleared, the way shines bright,
> In less, we glimpse the infinite,
> The sage, unburdened, light and free,
> Embodies Tao's simplicity.

Explanation:

Yu (◇), often translated as "excess" or "surplus," is a concept in Taoist philosophy that represents unnecessary complications, indulgences, or attachments that cloud our connection to the Tao. The principle of being without Yu encourages a life of simplicity, moderation, and clarity.

In the Tao Te Ching, Lao Tzu frequently warns against the dangers of excess:

"There is no greater sin than desire,

No greater curse than discontent,

No greater misfortune than wanting something for oneself.

Therefore he who knows that enough is enough will always have enough."

This passage highlights the Taoist view that many of our problems stem from wanting more than we need, or from complicating things unnecessarily. By letting go of excess, we can find contentment and align ourselves more closely with the natural simplicity of the Tao.

Being without Yu doesn't mean living in austere deprivation. Rather, it's about recognizing what is truly necessary and valuable, and not being swayed by superfluous desires or complications. It's about finding the right balance – having enough without being burdened by excess.

This principle is closely related to the Taoist concept of pu (◇), often translated as "simplicity" or "the uncarved block." Both ideas point to a state of natural simplicity that is uncluttered by unnecessary embellishments or artificial complexities.

Modern Application:

The principle of being without Yu offers valuable insights for our often excess-driven modern lives:

1. Minimalism: Embracing simplicity in our material possessions can lead to greater clarity and freedom.

2. Time Management: Eliminating unnecessary activities and commitments can help us focus on what's truly important.

3. Mental Clarity: Reducing mental clutter and information overload can lead to clearer thinking and decision-making.

4. Stress Reduction: Simplifying our lives and expectations can significantly reduce stress and anxiety.

5. Sustainability: Consuming less and avoiding excess aligns with more environmentally sustainable practices.

6. Relationships: Focusing on the quality rather than quantity of our relationships can lead to deeper, more meaningful connections.

7. Work-Life Balance: Avoiding the excesses of overwork can lead to a more harmonious and fulfilling life.

8. Financial Wellbeing: Practicing moderation in spending and avoiding unnecessary purchases can lead to greater financial stability and freedom.

Practical steps might include:

- Decluttering your physical space, keeping only what is necessary or truly meaningful
- Practicing mindfulness to become aware of when you're engaging in excess (in thoughts, actions, or consumption)
- Before making a purchase, pausing to consider whether it's truly necessary or valuable
- Simplifying your schedule by eliminating non-essential commitments
- Practicing gratitude for what you already have, rather than always seeking more
- Experimenting with periods of fasting (from food, social media, shopping, etc.) to reset your sense of what's enough
- In your work or creative projects, focusing on the essential elements and removing unnecessary complications
- Regularly reviewing your possessions, activities, and commitments to ensure they still serve you well

Reflection Questions:

1. In what areas of your life do you tend towards excess? How does this excess affect your wellbeing and peace of mind?

2. Can you recall a time when having less actually led to greater satisfaction or clarity? What did this experience teach you?

3. What fears or beliefs might be driving you to accumulate or indulge in excess?

4. How might your life change if you consistently chose simplicity over complexity, or enough

over more?

5. What would "enough" look like in different areas of your life (possessions, work, relationships, etc.)?

Remember, being without Yu is not about depriving yourself or living an austere life. It's about finding the sweet spot of sufficiency – having what you need and appreciating what you have, without being burdened by excess. As you explore this concept, pay attention to moments when simplicity brings a sense of peace or clarity. These can be guideposts as you navigate towards a life of greater balance and alignment with the Tao.

Chapter 25: Being from Da (Greatness)

In vastness of the Tao we find,

    True greatness of the sage's mind,

    Not grand in ego's fleeting light,

    But in alignment with what's right.

    Da's essence, humble yet profound,

    In cosmic dance, we're heaven-bound,

    The sage, embracing all that's small,

    Reflects the greatness in us all.

Explanation:

Da (大), often translated as "greatness" or "bigness," is a concept in Taoist philosophy that goes beyond mere size or importance. In Taoist thought, true greatness is not about personal aggrandizement or worldly success, but about aligning oneself with the vast, all-encompassing nature of the Tao.

In the Tao Te Ching, Lao Tzu speaks of greatness in paradoxical terms:

"The great Tao flows everywhere, both to the left and to the right.

The ten thousand things depend upon it; it holds nothing back.

It fulfills its purpose silently and makes no claim."

This passage illustrates that true greatness, like the Tao itself, is all-pervasive yet humble. It nourishes and supports all things without seeking recognition or reward.

The Taoist understanding of Da often involves a reversal of conventional thinking. Instead of striving to be great in the eyes of the world, the sage cultivates inner greatness through humility, simplicity, and alignment with the Tao. This greatness is not about standing above others, but about embracing one's place within the vast interconnected web of existence.

Importantly, Da in Taoist thought is not separate from its apparent opposite, xiao (小), or smallness. The sage understands that greatness and smallness are relative and interdependent. By embracing the small and humble, one paradoxically aligns with the greatest force in the universe - the Tao itself.

Modern Application:

The Taoist concept of Da offers valuable insights for our achievement-oriented modern lives:

1. Leadership: True greatness in leadership comes from serving others and the greater good, not from personal power or status.

2. Personal Growth: Focusing on inner development and alignment with deeper principles, rather than external markers of success.

3. Environmental Awareness: Recognizing our place within the vast ecosystem of Earth can inspire more responsible and humble behavior.

4. Creativity: Great creative works often come from embracing simplicity and aligning with universal themes.

5. Problem Solving: Approaching problems with humility and an awareness of their place in the larger context can lead to more effective solutions.

6. Relationships: Cultivating greatness in relationships through deep listening, empathy, and selfless action.

7. Career Development: Defining success not just by personal advancement, but by one's positive impact on others and the world.

8. Stress Management: Finding peace in aligning with something greater than oneself, rather than constantly striving for personal greatness.

Practical steps might include:

- Practicing mindfulness to cultivate awareness of your connection to the larger world
- Engaging in acts of service without seeking recognition
- Studying nature to understand principles of interconnectedness and natural harmony
- Reflecting on your life goals and how they align with broader principles of harmony and balance
- Practicing humility by acknowledging your limitations and the contributions of others
- Seeking out perspectives and experiences that expand your understanding of the world
- In your work or creative pursuits, focusing on how you can contribute to the greater good
- Regularly expressing gratitude for the vast network of people and natural systems that support your life

Reflection Questions:

1. How does your current understanding of greatness align with or differ from the Taoist concept of Da?

2. Can you recall a time when you experienced a sense of connection to something vastly greater than yourself? How did this experience affect you?

3. In what ways might striving for conventional greatness be limiting your alignment with the Tao?

4. How might embracing humility and simplicity paradoxically lead to greater fulfillment or effectiveness in your life?

5. Reflect on someone you consider truly great. How do they embody the Taoist understanding of Da?

Remember, cultivating Da is not about becoming superior to others or achieving worldly success. It's about aligning yourself with the vast, interconnected nature of the Tao and finding your place within it. As you explore this concept, notice how moments of true greatness often come when you're least focused on yourself and most connected to the larger flow of life. The path to Da is one of expansion through humility, of finding the universe in a grain of sand.

Chapter 26: Being Jing (Calmly)

In stillness, wisdom's waters clear,
    As Jing brings truth and insight near,
    Not frozen, stagnant, or inert,
    But calm amidst life's ebb and spurt.
    The sage, in tranquil poise abides,
    While chaos all around subsides,
    For in the eye of life's grand storm,
    Lies peace that's Tao's enduring form.

Explanation:

Jing (◈), often translated as "stillness" or "calmness," is a central concept in Taoist philosophy. It refers to a state of inner tranquility and clarity that allows one to perceive and act in harmony with the Tao. This calmness is not a passive or lifeless state, but a dynamic stillness full of potential and awareness.

In the Tao Te Ching, Lao Tzu emphasizes the importance of cultivating stillness:

"Be still.

Stillness reveals the secrets of eternity.

Eternity embraces the all-possible.

The all-possible leads to a vision of oneness.

A vision of oneness brings about universal love."

This passage suggests that through cultivating inner stillness, we can access deeper levels of wisdom and connection with the universe.

Jing is not about escaping from the world or suppressing our experiences. Rather, it's about developing a calm center within ourselves that remains steady amidst the fluctuations of life. From this place of inner calm, we can respond to situations more clearly and effectively, without being swept away by emotional reactions or external pressures.

Modern Application:

The principle of Jing offers valuable insights for our often hectic and overstimulating modern lives:

1. Stress Management: Cultivating inner calmness can significantly reduce stress and anxiety.

2. Decision Making: A calm mind can lead to clearer, more balanced decisions.

3. Relationships: Maintaining inner calm can help navigate interpersonal conflicts more

effectively.

4. Creativity: Moments of stillness often give rise to creative insights and solutions.

5. Productivity: Calm focus can enhance efficiency and the quality of our work.

6. Health: Practices that promote calmness can have numerous physical and mental health benefits.

7. Leadership: Leaders who embody calmness can provide stability and clear direction in challenging times.

8. Self-awareness: Inner stillness allows for deeper self-reflection and understanding.

Practical steps might include:

- Practicing meditation or mindfulness to cultivate inner stillness
- Creating regular moments of quiet in your daily routine
- Learning breath-work techniques to calm the mind and body
- Simplifying your environment to reduce external stimulation
- Practicing pausing before reacting in stressful situations
- Engaging in activities that promote a sense of flow and inner calm, like tai chi or painting
- Regularly spending time in nature to absorb its natural calmness
- Limiting exposure to sources of agitation, like excessive news or social media

Reflection Questions:

1. When do you feel most calm and centered in your life? What characterizes these moments?

2. How might cultivating more inner stillness change your response to challenges in your life?

3. In what ways does the noise and busyness of modern life affect your inner state? How can you create more space for calm?

4. Reflect on a time when being calm helped you handle a difficult situation. What did this teach you?

5. How might your relationships and work change if you consistently operated from a place of inner calm?

Chapter 27: Being by Neizhao (Inner Light)

Within us shines a guiding light,
    Neizhao, our inner sight,
    Not blinded by the world's facade,
    But lit by wisdom's living rod.
    The sage, attuned to this deep glow,
    Lets inner truth direct the show,
    For in our depths, when all goes still,
    The Tao's own light our beings fill.

Explanation:

Neizhao (◇◇), which can be translated as "inner light" or "inner illumination," is a profound concept in Taoist philosophy. It refers to the innate wisdom and clarity that comes from within, rather than from external sources of knowledge or guidance. This inner light is seen as a direct connection to the Tao itself, providing intuitive understanding and guidance.

In Taoist thought, cultivating Neizhao involves turning our attention inward, away from the distractions and illusions of the external world. It's about trusting our inherent capacity for wisdom and insight, rather than always seeking answers from outside ourselves.

The Tao Te Ching alludes to this concept in various ways:

"Knowing others is intelligence;

knowing yourself is true wisdom.

Mastering others is strength;

mastering yourself is true power."

This passage highlights the importance of self-knowledge and inner cultivation, which are key aspects of developing Neizhao.

The concept of inner light suggests that true understanding comes not just from intellectual knowledge, but from a deeper, more intuitive form of knowing. By cultivating this inner light, we can navigate life's challenges with greater wisdom and alignment with the Tao.

Modern Application:

The principle of Neizhao offers valuable insights for our often externally-focused modern lives:

1. Self-trust: Developing confidence in our own intuition and inner wisdom.

2. Decision Making: Using our inner light to guide choices, rather than always relying on external advice.

3. Authenticity: Living more genuinely by aligning with our inner truth.

4. Creativity: Tapping into our inner light as a source of original ideas and inspiration.

5. Personal Growth: Focusing on inner development rather than just acquiring external knowledge.

6. Resilience: Finding an inner source of strength and guidance during challenging times.

7. Leadership: Leading from a place of inner clarity and conviction.

8. Spiritual Practice: Deepening our spiritual life by connecting with our inner light.

Practical steps might include:

- Practicing regular meditation or self-reflection to connect with your inner light
- Journaling to explore your inner thoughts and intuitions
- Taking time for solitude to hear your inner voice more clearly
- Before making decisions, checking in with your inner sense of what feels right
- Engaging in creative activities that allow you to express your inner truth
- Practicing saying "no" to things that don't align with your inner wisdom
- Learning to distinguish between the voice of your inner light and that of your ego or conditioned responses
- Regularly asking yourself, "What do I truly know from within?"

Reflection Questions:

1. When have you felt most in touch with your inner light or wisdom? What were the circumstances?

2. How often do you trust your own inner guidance versus seeking external validation or advice?

3. What practices or activities help you connect more deeply with your inner light?

4. How might your life change if you consistently made decisions based on your inner light rather than external pressures or expectations?

5. In what areas of your life do you find it most challenging to trust your inner wisdom? Why might this be?

Remember, both Jing (calmness) and Neizhao (inner light) are interconnected aspects of Taoist practice. Cultivating inner calm often allows our inner light to shine more brightly, while connecting with our inner light can bring a profound sense of calm. As you explore these concepts, notice how they support and enhance each other in your journey of self-discovery and alignment with the Tao.

Chapter 28: Being with De (Virtuously)

Not rules or laws, but inner grace,

De guides us through time and space,

A power born of Tao's embrace,

In every act, we find its trace.

The sage, aligned with virtue's flow,

Needs not to preach or praise or show,

For in De's silent, gentle might,

All beings turn toward the light.

Explanation:

De (◈), often translated as "virtue" or "power," is a central concept in Taoist philosophy. Unlike conventional notions of morality or goodness, De in Taoism refers to the innate power that arises from one's alignment with the Tao. It's not about following external rules, but about cultivating and expressing one's true nature in harmony with the fundamental principles of the universe.

In the Tao Te Ching, Lao Tzu often describes De as a kind of potency or efficacy that comes from being in accord with the Tao:

"The person of superior virtue is not virtuous, and that is why he has virtue. The person of inferior virtue never strays from virtue, and that is why he lacks virtue."

This paradoxical statement suggests that true virtue (De) is not about consciously trying to be good, but about naturally and spontaneously expressing one's alignment with the Tao.

Modern Application:

1. Ethics: Developing an innate sense of right action rather than following rigid moral codes.

2. Leadership: Influencing others through embodiment of principles rather than through force or manipulation.

3. Personal Growth: Focusing on aligning with one's true nature rather than trying to conform to external standards.

4. Relationships: Cultivating genuine care and integrity in interactions with others.

5. Career: Finding work that allows for the natural expression of one's De.

Practical steps:

- Regular self-reflection to understand your true nature and values
- Practicing authenticity in your daily interactions

- Observing the natural world to learn about effortless virtue
- Cultivating mindfulness to act from a place of alignment rather than reaction
- Regularly reassessing your actions: do they flow naturally from your authentic self?

Reflection Questions:

1. When do you feel you're most in alignment with your true nature?

2. How might your approach to ethics and morality change if you focused on cultivating De rather than following rules?

3. In what ways do you currently express your De in your daily life?

4. How might embracing the concept of De change your approach to personal growth and development?

5. Can you recall a time when you witnessed someone embodying De? How did it affect those around them?

Chapter 29: Being by Tian (Natural Law)

In heaven's way, we find our guide,
    Tian's patterns, in which we abide,
    Not distant force, but close at hand,
    In every leaf and grain of sand.
    The sage, attuned to nature's song,
    Knows right from wrong, and weak from strong,
    For in Tian's endless ebb and flow,
    The path of Tao we come to know.

Explanation:

Tian (◈), often translated as "Heaven" or "Nature," is a fundamental concept in Chinese philosophy, including Taoism. In Taoist thought, Tian represents the natural order of the universe, the inherent principles that govern all things. It's not a personified deity, but rather the spontaneous, self-organizing intelligence of the cosmos.

Lao Tzu refers to Tian in the Tao Te Ching:

"Humans follow the Earth, Earth follows Heaven, Heaven follows the Tao, and the Tao follows what is natural."

This passage illustrates the Taoist view that the highest wisdom lies in aligning ourselves with the natural principles of the universe.

Modern Application:

1. Environmental Stewardship: Understanding and working with natural processes rather than against them.

2. Personal Ethics: Deriving principles of right action from observation of natural patterns.

3. Science and Technology: Developing innovations that are in harmony with natural laws.

4. Health and Wellness: Aligning our lifestyles with natural rhythms and principles.

5. Governance: Creating systems and policies that reflect natural laws of balance and interdependence.

Practical steps:

- Spending time in nature, observing its patterns and cycles
- Studying ecology and systems thinking to understand natural laws
- Aligning daily routines with natural rhythms (e.g., sleep-wake cycles)

- In decision-making, considering the wider impact and natural consequences
- Practicing biomimicry in problem-solving, looking to nature for solutions

Reflection Questions:
1. How aligned do you feel your current lifestyle is with natural rhythms and principles?
2. Can you think of a time when going against natural principles led to difficulties in your life?
3. In what ways might a deeper understanding of Tian change your approach to challenges or goals?
4. How might society change if it were more aligned with the concept of Tian?
5. What aspects of nature do you find most instructive or inspiring for your personal life?

Chapter 30: Being Without Li (Force)

In gentleness, true strength resides,

As without force, the sage abides,

Not weak or frail, but deeply strong,

Li's push and pull we move along.

The Tao works not by might or power,

But like the opening of a flower,

In yielding grace, we find our way,

As night gives way to gentle day.

Explanation:

Li (◈), typically translated as "force" or "strength," is a concept that Taoism often advises against when it comes to interacting with the world. The Taoist ideal is to accomplish things without resorting to forceful action, instead working in harmony with the natural flow of circumstances.

Lao Tzu expresses this idea in the Tao Te Ching:

"The softest thing in the universe overcomes the hardest thing in the universe. That without substance can enter where there is no room. Hence I know the value of non-action."

This passage highlights the Taoist preference for soft, yielding approaches over hard, forceful ones.

Modern Application:

1. Conflict Resolution: Using diplomacy and understanding rather than force or coercion.

2. Leadership: Guiding through inspiration and example rather than authority and control.

3. Personal Growth: Allowing change to happen naturally rather than forcing development.

4. Problem Solving: Finding solutions that work with existing conditions rather than imposing external force.

5. Relationships: Cultivating connections through acceptance and understanding rather than trying to change others.

Practical steps:

- Practicing patience in difficult situations, allowing solutions to emerge naturally
- Learning the art of persuasion and influence without coercion
- In conflicts, focusing on understanding all perspectives before taking action
- Cultivating flexibility and adaptability in your approach to challenges

- Regularly reflecting on where you might be using unnecessary force in your life

Reflection Questions:

1. In what areas of your life do you tend to use force or push against resistance?

2. Can you recall a situation where a gentle approach was more effective than a forceful one?

3. How might your relationships change if you practiced being without Li more consistently?

4. What fears or beliefs might be driving you to use force in certain situations?

5. How could the principle of being without Li change your approach to your goals and ambitions?

Remember, these Taoist principles - De (Virtue), Tian (Natural Law), and being without Li (Force) - are interconnected aspects of living in harmony with the Tao. As you explore these concepts, notice how they support and inform each other, offering a holistic approach to navigating life with wisdom and grace.

Chapter 31: Being Without Bing (Weapons)

In peace, not war, true power lies,

    As Bing falls away, wisdom rises,

    Not weak or defenseless, but strong,

    In harmony, where all belong.

    The sage finds strength in open hands,

    In bridges built, not borderlands,

    For in the absence of the sword,

    The Tao's deep peace can be restored.

Explanation:

Bing (◇), typically translated as "weapons" or "military," represents force, violence, and conflict in Taoist philosophy. The Tao Te Ching advocates for minimizing the use of weapons and military force, seeing them as contrary to the harmonious way of the Tao.

Lao Tzu expresses this in Chapter 31 of the Tao Te Ching:

"Weapons are instruments of fear; they are not a wise man's tools.

He uses them only when he has no choice.

Peace and quiet are dear to his heart,

And victory no cause for rejoicing."

This passage highlights the Taoist view that weapons and violence should be absolute last resorts, used reluctantly if at all.

Modern Application:

1. Conflict Resolution: Prioritizing diplomatic and peaceful solutions over force.

2. Personal Relationships: Avoiding aggression and cultivating understanding in interactions.

3. Self-Defense: Focusing on de-escalation and avoidance rather than confrontation.

4. Leadership: Guiding through inspiration and example rather than force or threat.

5. Social Activism: Promoting change through non-violent means.

Practical steps:

- Practicing non-violent communication in conflicts
- Learning meditation or mindfulness to manage aggressive impulses
- Studying the history and effectiveness of non-violent movements
- In disagreements, focusing on finding common ground rather than "winning"

- Regularly reflecting on where you might be using "weapons" (physical or verbal) in your life

Reflection Questions:

1. In what ways do you use "weapons" (literal or metaphorical) in your daily life?

2. How might your approach to conflicts change if you embraced the principle of being without Bing?

3. Can you recall a situation where a non-violent approach led to a better outcome than force would have?

4. What fears or beliefs might be driving you to rely on "weapons" in certain situations?

5. How could the principle of being without Bing change your view on larger societal issues?

Chapter 32: Being the De of Dao

In virtue's flow, the Tao we find,
    As De and Dao are intertwined,
    Not separate paths, but one true way,
    In every act, the Tao holds sway.
    The sage embodies cosmic grace,
    In every step and every place,
    For in the dance of De and Tao,
    We learn to be, we learn to now.

Explanation:

The De of Dao (��) represents the manifestation or expression of the Tao in the world. While the Tao is the underlying principle of the universe, De is how this principle manifests in individual beings and actions. It's the active expression of one's alignment with the Tao.

In the Tao Te Ching, Lao Tzu often speaks of the relationship between Tao and De:

"The Tao gives birth to all beings,

nourishes them, maintains them,

cares for them, comforts them, protects them,

takes them back to itself,

creating without possessing,

acting without expecting,

guiding without interfering.

That is why love of the Tao

is in the very nature of things."

This passage illustrates how De (virtue) naturally flows from alignment with the Tao.

Modern Application:

1. Ethical Living: Deriving one's ethics from alignment with universal principles rather than external rules.

2. Personal Development: Focusing on cultivating inner virtue rather than acquiring external markers of success.

3. Leadership: Leading by embodiment of principles rather than through force or manipulation.

4. Creativity: Allowing creative expression to flow naturally from one's alignment with deeper principles.

5. Relationships: Cultivating genuine care and integrity in interactions with others.

Practical steps:

- Regular self-reflection to understand how your actions align with deeper principles
- Practicing mindfulness to act from a place of alignment rather than reaction
- Studying nature to observe how De manifests in the natural world
- In decision-making, considering what action would be most in harmony with the Tao
- Regularly asking yourself, "How can I express the De of Dao in this situation?"

Reflection Questions:

1. How do you currently express the De of Dao in your daily life?

2. Can you recall a time when you felt completely aligned with the Tao? What characterized this experience?

3. In what areas of your life do you find it most challenging to manifest De?

4. How might your approach to personal growth change if you focused on cultivating the De of Dao?

5. What societal changes might occur if more people lived in accordance with the De of Dao?

Chapter 33: Being Zhi (Self-Mastery)

In self-control, true freedom's found,
    As Zhi takes root on inner ground,
    Not rigid rules or iron will,
    But flow that lets the Tao distill.
    The sage, in mastery of the soul,
    Finds parts and whole in cosmic role,
    For in the art of self-command,
    We learn to flow, we learn to stand.

Explanation:

Zhi (◈) in Taoist philosophy refers to self-mastery or self-control. However, it's important to understand that this isn't about rigid self-discipline or suppression of natural instincts. Rather, it's about aligning oneself with the Tao so completely that one's actions naturally flow in harmony with it.

The Tao Te Ching speaks to this idea of mastery:

"Mastering others is strength;

mastering yourself is true power."

This passage suggests that true power comes not from controlling external circumstances, but from achieving inner harmony and self-understanding.

Modern Application:

1. Emotional Intelligence: Developing the ability to understand and manage one's emotions.

2. Habit Formation: Cultivating beneficial habits that align with one's deeper values.

3. Decision Making: Making choices from a place of inner clarity rather than external pressures.

4. Stress Management: Developing inner resources to remain calm and centered in challenging situations.

5. Personal Growth: Focusing on inner development rather than trying to control external circumstances.

Practical steps:

- Practicing mindfulness to become more aware of your thoughts and impulses
- Engaging in regular self-reflection to understand your motivations and patterns
- Studying and applying principles of habit formation and behavior change

- Practicing delayed gratification in small ways to build self-control
- Regularly setting and working towards personal growth goals

Reflection Questions:

1. In what areas of your life do you feel you have the most self-mastery? The least?

2. How does your understanding of self-mastery align with or differ from the Taoist concept of Zhi?

3. Can you recall a time when self-mastery led to a positive outcome in your life?

4. How might your life change if you consistently practiced Zhi in all areas?

5. What obstacles do you face in developing greater self-mastery?

Remember, these Taoist principles - being without Bing (Weapons), embodying the De of Dao, and cultivating Zhi (Self-Mastery) - are interconnected aspects of living in harmony with the Tao. As you explore these concepts, notice how they support and inform each other, offering a holistic approach to personal development and alignment with the natural order of the universe.

Chapter 34: Being Dao (The Way)

In every breath, in every move,

    We dance the Dao, our spirits prove,

    Not distant path, but here and now,

    In being Dao, we learn to bow.

    To life's great flow, we sync our stride,

    As sage and student side by side,

    For in the way of wu wei's art,

    We find the Dao in every heart.

Explanation:

Being Dao (◇) is the ultimate aim of Taoist practice. It means aligning oneself so completely with the fundamental nature of the universe that one becomes an embodiment of the Tao itself. This isn't about achieving a static state, but about flowing harmoniously with the ever-changing nature of existence.

Lao Tzu describes the Tao in the opening lines of the Tao Te Ching:

"The Tao that can be told is not the eternal Tao.

The name that can be named is not the eternal name."

This passage highlights the ineffable nature of the Tao, suggesting that truly being Dao goes beyond intellectual understanding or description.

Modern Application:

1. Mindfulness: Cultivating present-moment awareness to align with the flow of life.

2. Adaptability: Developing the flexibility to move with change rather than resist it.

3. Holistic Thinking: Seeing the interconnections in all aspects of life and work.

4. Ethical Living: Deriving one's ethics from alignment with natural principles.

5. Creativity: Allowing ideas and actions to arise spontaneously from one's connection with the Tao.

Practical steps:

- Practicing mindfulness meditation to cultivate present-moment awareness
- Regularly spending time in nature to observe and align with natural rhythms
- Studying systems thinking to understand interconnections in life
- Practicing wu wei (non-action) in daily activities

- Regularly reflecting on how your actions align with the flow of life

Reflection Questions:
1. When do you feel most aligned with the flow of life?
2. How might your daily life change if you consistently embodied the Tao?
3. What obstacles do you face in aligning more fully with the Tao?
4. Can you recall a time when you felt you were effortlessly "being Dao"?
5. How does the concept of "being Dao" challenge or support your current worldview?

Chapter 35: Being Beyond Yu (Worldly Pleasures)

Beyond the fleeting joys we chase,
Lies deeper bliss in Tao's embrace,
Not austere life or pleasure's drain,
But balance found in joy's refrain.
The sage, content with simple things,
Knows peace that true detachment brings,
For in releasing worldly ties,
We find where lasting treasure lies.

Explanation:

Being beyond Yu (◈), or worldly desires and pleasures, is a key aspect of Taoist practice. This doesn't mean complete renunciation of pleasure, but rather not being controlled by desires or attached to fleeting sensations. It's about finding a deeper, more lasting contentment that comes from alignment with the Tao.

In the Tao Te Ching, Lao Tzu writes:

"There is no greater sin than desire,

No greater curse than discontent,

No greater misfortune than wanting something for oneself.

Therefore he who knows that enough is enough will always have enough."

This passage highlights the Taoist view that excessive desire leads to suffering, while contentment brings peace.

Modern Application:

1. Mindful Consumption: Being more conscious about what we consume and why.

2. Contentment: Cultivating satisfaction with what we have rather than always wanting more.

3. Stress Reduction: Letting go of the pressure to constantly seek pleasure or avoid discomfort.

4. Financial Wellbeing: Developing a healthier relationship with money and material possessions.

5. Relationships: Focusing on deeper connections rather than superficial pleasures.

Practical steps:

- Practicing gratitude for what you already have
- Engaging in periods of voluntary simplicity or fasting from certain pleasures
- Mindfulness meditation to observe desires without automatically acting on them

- Regularly reflecting on what truly brings you lasting satisfaction
- Exploring non-materialistic sources of joy and fulfillment

Reflection Questions:

1. What worldly pleasures do you find yourself most attached to?

2. Can you recall a time when letting go of a desire led to greater peace or satisfaction?

3. How might your life change if you were less driven by the pursuit of pleasure?

4. What fears or beliefs might be driving your attachment to certain worldly pleasures?

5. How does the idea of being beyond Yu challenge or support your current life goals?

Chapter 36: Being in Yin (Obscurity)

In shadows deep, where few dare tread,
The sage finds strength in quiet stead,
Not seeking fame or fortune's light,
But wisdom born in yin's soft night.
In humble deeds and silent ways,
We find the power of hidden days,
For in obscurity's embrace,
We touch the Tao's eternal grace.

Explanation:

Being in Yin (◇), or obscurity, is a Taoist principle that values the hidden, the subtle, and the understated. It suggests that true power and wisdom often lie in what is not obvious or celebrated. This concept encourages retreating from the limelight and finding strength in quietude and hiddenness.

Lao Tzu speaks to this in the Tao Te Ching:

"Those who know do not speak.

Those who speak do not know."

This passage highlights the Taoist preference for quiet wisdom over ostentatious display of knowledge.

Modern Application:

1. Humility: Cultivating the ability to work without need for recognition.

2. Inner Work: Focusing on personal growth rather than external achievements.

3. Leadership: Leading from behind, empowering others rather than seeking the spotlight.

4. Creativity: Finding inspiration and insight in quiet reflection and solitude.

5. Stress Reduction: Stepping back from the pressure of constant visibility and performance.

Practical steps:

- Practicing anonymity in good deeds
- Cultivating a rich inner life through reflection and meditation
- Seeking out periods of solitude and retreat
- Learning to listen more than you speak
- Finding ways to contribute that don't require public recognition

Reflection Questions:

1. How comfortable are you with being in the background or unrecognized?

2. Can you recall a time when working in obscurity led to unexpected benefits?

3. How might embracing Yin change your approach to your work or personal goals?

4. What fears or beliefs might be driving a need for recognition or visibility in your life?

5. How could the principle of being in Yin enhance your personal growth and wisdom?

Remember, these Taoist principles - Being Dao, Being Beyond Yu, and Being in Yin - are interconnected aspects of living in harmony with the Tao. As you explore these concepts, notice how they support and inform each other, offering a holistic approach to finding peace, wisdom, and alignment in life.

Chapter 37: Being in Pu (Simplicity)

In simplicity's pure embrace,
    We find the Tao's enduring grace,
    Not barren, dull, or unrefined,
    But essence of the sage's mind.
    Pu's uncarved block, potential's store,
    Opens to life an boundless door,
    For in the simple and the plain,
    We touch the Tao's eternal reign.

Explanation:

Pu (⟡), often translated as "simplicity" or "the uncarved block," is a fundamental concept in Taoism. It represents a state of pure potential, unshaped by human intervention or desire. Pu is about returning to our original nature, free from unnecessary complications or artificial embellishments.

In the Tao Te Ching, Lao Tzu alludes to this concept:

"When your work is done, then withdraw. This is the way of heaven."

This passage suggests that the natural state, unadorned and simple, is the most aligned with the Tao.

Modern Application:

1. Minimalism: Embracing a simpler lifestyle with fewer possessions and commitments.
2. Authenticity: Striving to be one's true self, free from societal expectations.
3. Problem Solving: Approaching challenges with a fresh, uncomplicated perspective.
4. Creativity: Finding inspiration in simplicity and basic forms.
5. Stress Reduction: Simplifying one's life to reduce complexity and overwhelm.

Practical steps:

- Decluttering your physical space and digital life
- Practicing mindfulness to observe thoughts without elaboration
- Simplifying your daily routines and commitments
- Engaging in creative activities that start with basic forms (like sculpture or drawing)
- Regularly asking yourself, "Is this necessary?" in various aspects of life

Reflection Questions:

1. In what areas of your life do you feel most cluttered or overcomplicated?

2. How might embracing Pu change your approach to personal growth or creativity?

3. Can you recall a time when simplifying led to a breakthrough or insight?

4. What fears or beliefs might be preventing you from embracing greater simplicity in your life?

5. How could the principle of Pu enhance your relationships or work?

Chapter 38: Being within Xing (Own Nature)

Within our depths, a truth resides,
    As Xing, our nature, gently guides,
    Not forced or feigned, but pure and true,
    In every thought and all we do.
    The sage, aligned with inner light,
    Needs not to strive or prove what's right,
    For in our nature's quiet call,
    We find the Tao that moves us all.

Explanation:

Xing (◇) refers to one's inherent nature or essence. In Taoist philosophy, it's believed that each being has its own unique nature that, when recognized and followed, leads to harmony with the Tao. Being within Xing is about aligning with and expressing this authentic nature rather than conforming to external expectations.

Zhuangzi, another key Taoist philosopher, often spoke about the importance of following one's nature:

"Flow with whatever may happen and let your mind be free. Stay centered by accepting whatever you are doing. This is the ultimate."

This quote emphasizes the importance of staying true to one's nature amidst life's changes.

Modern Application:

1. Self-Discovery: Engaging in practices that help you understand your true nature.

2. Career Choices: Aligning work with your innate talents and inclinations.

3. Relationships: Being authentic in your interactions with others.

4. Personal Growth: Developing in ways that are true to your essence rather than following prescribed paths.

5. Decision Making: Making choices that resonate with your inner nature.

Practical steps:

- Regular self-reflection to understand your natural inclinations and values
- Experimenting with different activities to discover what truly resonates with you
- Practicing saying no to things that don't align with your nature
- Seeking feedback from trusted others about when you seem most authentic

- Regularly asking yourself, "Is this true to who I really am?"

Reflection Questions:

1. When do you feel most authentically yourself?

2. How aligned is your current lifestyle with your true nature?

3. What aspects of your nature do you find most challenging to express or accept?

4. How might your life change if you consistently honored your Xing?

5. What societal expectations or personal beliefs might be preventing you from fully expressing your nature?

Chapter 39: Being He (Wholeness)

In unity, all parts combine,
    As He reveals the grand design,
    Not fragmented, not torn apart,
    But whole in mind and whole in heart.
    The sage sees one where others split,
    In cosmic dance, all pieces fit,
    For in the whole, we come to see,
    The Tao's profound simplicity.

Explanation:

He (◈), often translated as "harmony" or "wholeness," is a concept that emphasizes the unity and interconnectedness of all things.

In Taoist thought, true understanding comes from seeing the whole rather than focusing solely on individual parts. It's about recognizing the underlying unity in apparent diversity.

The Tao Te Ching touches on this concept:

"The Tao is the whole. From it, all things arise and to it all return."

This passage highlights the Taoist view of the fundamental unity of all existence.

Modern Application:

1. Holistic Thinking: Approaching problems by considering the entire system rather than isolated parts.

2. Conflict Resolution: Seeking solutions that benefit the whole rather than favoring one side.

3. Health and Wellness: Adopting a holistic approach to wellbeing that considers mind, body, and spirit.

4. Environmental Awareness: Recognizing our interconnectedness with nature and all living beings.

5. Personal Growth: Developing all aspects of oneself in balance rather than overemphasizing certain areas.

Practical steps:

- Practicing systems thinking in your work or personal life
- Engaging in activities that connect you with nature and the larger world
- When facing conflicts, try to see from multiple perspectives

- Adopting holistic health practices that address physical, mental, and spiritual wellbeing
- Regularly reflecting on how your actions affect the larger whole of your community or environment

Reflection Questions:

1. In what areas of your life do you tend to see things as separate rather than interconnected?

2. How might embracing wholeness change your approach to current challenges?

3. Can you recall a time when seeing the bigger picture led to a breakthrough or resolution?

4. How does the concept of He challenge or support your current worldview?

5. What practices could you adopt to cultivate a greater sense of wholeness in your daily life?

Remember, these Taoist principles - Being in Pu (Simplicity), Being within Xing (Own Nature), and Being He (Wholeness) - are interconnected aspects of living in harmony with the Tao. As you explore these concepts, notice how they support and complement each other, offering a comprehensive approach to finding balance, authenticity, and unity in life.

Chapter 40: Being by Fan (Returning and Yielding)

In life's great cycle, ebb and flow,
    The sage learns when to come and go,
    Fan's wisdom teaches how to bend,
    To yield, return, and transcend.
    Not clinging tight to what we know,
    But letting come and letting go,
    For in return, we find our way,
    To Tao's eternal, present day.

Explanation:

Fan (◇) in Taoist philosophy represents the principle of return or reversal. It embodies the cyclical nature of existence and the idea that all things eventually return to their source. This concept also includes the notion of yielding or reversing course when meeting resistance, rather than pushing forward forcefully.

Lao Tzu speaks of this principle in the Tao Te Ching:

"Returning is the motion of the Tao.

Yielding is the way of the Tao."

This passage highlights the importance of aligning with natural cycles and knowing when to yield or return.

Modern Application:

1. Adaptability: Being flexible and willing to change course when faced with obstacles.

2. Stress Management: Knowing when to step back and regroup rather than pushing through exhaustion.

3. Problem Solving: Approaching issues from different angles, sometimes by "reversing" our thinking.

4. Personal Growth: Understanding that setbacks can be opportunities for returning to basics and rebuilding.

5. Environmental Sustainability: Recognizing the importance of recycling and returning resources to nature.

Practical steps:

- Practicing the art of yielding in conflicts or disagreements

- Incorporating regular periods of rest and reflection in your routine
- When stuck on a problem, try reversing your usual approach
- In personal development, periodically returning to foundational practices or principles
- Observing natural cycles (seasons, day/night) and aligning your activities with them

Reflection Questions:

1. When in your life have you benefited from yielding or returning rather than pushing forward?

2. How might embracing the principle of Fan change your approach to current challenges?

3. In what areas of your life might you need to 'return to the source' or basics?

4. How does the concept of cyclical return challenge or support your view of progress and growth?

5. What fears or beliefs might be preventing you from yielding when it would be beneficial?

Chapter 41: Being Beyond Xiang (Appearances)

Beyond the veil of what we see,
>Lies truth in deep reality,
>Not trapped by form or fleeting shape,
>But essence that cannot escape.
>The sage looks past the surface show,
>To touch the current's undertow,
>For in the depths beyond Xiang's mask,
>We find the Tao, our truest task.

Explanation:

Being beyond Xiang (◇), or appearances, is about recognizing that the surface level of things often conceals a deeper reality. In Taoist thought, true wisdom comes from looking beyond the obvious and understanding the underlying essence of things.

Lao Tzu alludes to this concept in the Tao Te Ching:

"The Tao that can be told is not the eternal Tao.

The name that can be named is not the eternal name."

This passage suggests that the true nature of reality goes beyond what can be perceived or described.

Modern Application:

1. Critical Thinking: Looking beyond surface-level information to understand deeper truths.

2. Personal Relationships: Seeing beyond appearances to understand people's true nature and motivations.

3. Self-Understanding: Recognizing that our self-image may not reflect our true essence.

4. Media Literacy: Being aware of how appearances can be manipulated, especially in the digital age.

5. Scientific Inquiry: Pushing beyond apparent phenomena to understand underlying principles.

Practical steps:

- Practicing mindfulness to observe thoughts and appearances without attachment
- Regularly questioning your first impressions and assumptions
- Engaging in deep listening, focusing on understanding rather than responding
- Exploring meditation practices that cultivate awareness of formless reality

- In decision-making, looking beyond immediate appearances to consider long-term and systemic effects

Reflection Questions:
1. When have you been misled by appearances in your life? What did you learn from this?
2. How might your relationships change if you consistently looked beyond surface appearances?
3. In what areas of your life do you tend to get caught up in appearances or form?
4. How does the idea of a reality beyond appearances challenge or support your worldview?
5. What practices could help you cultivate a deeper perception beyond Xiang in your daily life?

Chapter 42: Being by Rong (Melting into Harmony)

In life's grand symphony we play,
As Rong guides us in Tao's way,
Not standing out, but blending in,
In harmony, we truly win.
The sage, attuned to cosmic song,
Finds strength in where we all belong,
For in the melting of the soul,
We touch the Tao and become whole.

Explanation:

Rong (◇) represents the concept of melting or merging, particularly in the context of harmonizing with one's environment or with the Tao itself. It's about letting go of rigid boundaries of the self and flowing with the greater whole.

While not directly quoted in the Tao Te Ching, this concept aligns closely with Taoist ideas of wu wei and harmony with nature. As Lao Tzu says:

"The best way to live is to be like water. Water is good; it benefits all things and does not compete with them."

This passage illustrates the principle of harmonious integration that Rong embodies.

Modern Application:

1. Teamwork: Ability to collaborate effectively by aligning with the group's energy.

2. Cultural Adaptability: Skill in harmonizing with different cultural environments.

3. Ecological Awareness: Understanding our interconnectedness with nature and acting accordingly.

4. Conflict Resolution: Finding solutions that harmonize different viewpoints rather than promoting one over others.

5. Creativity: Allowing ideas to flow and merge, leading to novel combinations and innovations.

Practical steps:

- Practicing group activities that require synchronization (like choral singing or team sports)
- Spending time in nature, observing how different elements harmonize
- In conversations, focus on building upon others' ideas rather than asserting your own
- Experimenting with improvisational art or music to experience creative flow
- When facing conflicts, look for ways to blend different perspectives rather than choosing sides

Reflection Questions:

1. When have you experienced a sense of melting into harmony with your environment or others?

2. How might embracing Rong change your approach to relationships or teamwork?

3. In what areas of your life do you find it most challenging to 'melt' or harmonize?

4. How does the concept of Rong challenge or support your sense of individual identity?

5. What fears or beliefs might be preventing you from more fully harmonizing in certain situations?

Remember, these Taoist principles - Being by Fan (Returning and Yielding), Being Beyond Xiang (Appearances), and Being by Rong (Melting into Harmony) - are interconnected aspects of living in alignment with the Tao. As you explore these concepts, notice how they complement and reinforce each other, offering a multifaceted approach to navigating life with wisdom and grace.

Chapter 43: Being Rou (Softly)

In gentleness, true strength resides,
    As Rou through life serenely glides,
    Not weak or frail, but deeply strong,
    Like water's flow, it moves along.
    The sage, in softness, finds his might,
    Yielding, yet winning every fight,
    For in the supple and the meek,
    We find the power that all seek.

Explanation:

Rou (⟡), often translated as "softness" or "gentleness," is a key concept in Taoist philosophy. It represents a kind of strength that comes from flexibility and adaptability rather than rigid force. In Taoist thought, the soft and yielding are seen as ultimately stronger than the hard and inflexible.

Lao Tzu emphasizes this principle in the Tao Te Ching:

"The softest thing in the universe

Overcomes the hardest thing in the universe.

That without substance can enter where there is no room.

Hence I know the value of non-action."

This passage illustrates the paradoxical power of softness, which can overcome seemingly insurmountable obstacles through its ability to adapt and flow around resistance.

The concept of Rou is often exemplified in nature. Water, for instance, is soft and yielding, yet over time it can wear away even the hardest rock. A young sapling bends in the wind and survives, while the rigid old tree breaks. These natural metaphors highlight the strength and resilience inherent in softness.

In Taoist practice, cultivating Rou involves developing a mindset of flexibility and non-resistance. It's about learning to flow with circumstances rather than constantly fighting against them. This doesn't mean being passive or weak, but rather finding a way of engaging with the world that is both effective and harmonious.

Modern Application:

1. Conflict Resolution: Using diplomacy and understanding rather than force to resolve disputes.

2. Stress Management: Developing resilience through flexibility rather than rigid resistance to challenges.

3. Leadership: Leading through influence and inspiration rather than domination and control.

4. Personal Relationships: Cultivating empathy and adaptability in interactions with others.

5. Problem Solving: Approaching challenges with a flexible mindset, willing to adapt strategies as needed.

6. Physical Health: Understanding the importance of flexibility alongside strength in physical fitness.

7. Emotional Intelligence: Developing the ability to respond to emotions (both one's own and others') with gentleness and understanding.

8. Environmental Stewardship: Recognizing the power of gentle, persistent action in creating change.

Practical steps:

- Practicing soft martial arts like Tai Chi or Aikido to experience physical softness as strength
- In conflicts, experimenting with yielding or redirecting energy rather than meeting force with force
- Incorporating flexibility exercises into your physical fitness routine
- When faced with obstacles, brainstorming ways to flow around them rather than always trying to push through
- Practicing active listening in conversations, softening your stance to truly understand others
- In problem-solving, trying multiple gentle approaches rather than one forceful method
- Observing nature to find examples of how softness and flexibility lead to resilience and longevity
- Regularly reflecting on areas in your life where you might be too rigid and could benefit from more softness

Reflection Questions:

1. Recall a time when being soft or flexible led to a better outcome than being rigid or forceful. What did this teach you?

2. In what areas of your life do you tend to be too hard or inflexible? How might cultivating Rou in these areas benefit you?

3. How does the idea of strength through softness challenge or support your current understanding of power and effectiveness?

4. Think of someone you know who embodies Rou. How does their softness manifest as strength in their life?

5. How might embracing Rou change your approach to current challenges or goals in your life?

6. What fears or beliefs might be preventing you from embracing softness in certain situations?

7. How could the principle of Rou enhance your relationships, both personal and professional?

Remember, cultivating Rou is not about becoming weak or passive, but about developing a kind of strength that is more adaptable and ultimately more resilient. As you explore this concept, pay attention to moments when yielding or being gentle feels more powerful than resisting or forcing. These can be opportunities to deepen your understanding and practice of Rou in your daily life.

Chapter 44: Being by Zhi Zhi (Knowing When to Stop)

In wisdom's realm, a truth resides,
    Knowing when to stem the tides,
    Zhi Zhi, the art of timely pause,
    Aligns our actions with Tao's laws.
    The sage, in knowing when to cease,
    Finds in restraint a deep release,
    For in the spaces where we wait,
    We touch the Tao's eternal state.

Explanation:

Zhi Zhi (◇◇), which can be translated as "knowing when to stop," is a subtle yet profound concept in Taoist philosophy. It embodies the wisdom of recognizing limits, understanding the right moment to cease action, and appreciating the value of restraint.

In the Tao Te Ching, Lao Tzu speaks directly to this principle:

"Knowing when you have enough is true wealth.

Knowing when to stop is necessary to preserve yourself from danger and exhaustion."

This passage highlights the importance of contentment and the wisdom of not overextending oneself. In Taoist thought, knowing when to stop is as important as knowing when to act. It's about finding the right balance between action and non-action, effort and rest.

The concept of Zhi Zhi is closely related to the Taoist ideal of wu wei, or effortless action. By knowing when to stop, we avoid wasting energy on unnecessary efforts and align ourselves more closely with the natural flow of the Tao. This principle applies not just to physical actions, but also to mental and emotional processes – knowing when to stop thinking, worrying, or desiring.

In nature, we see examples of Zhi Zhi in the changing of seasons, the ebb and flow of tides, and the cycles of growth and rest in plants. These natural rhythms demonstrate the importance of timely cessation as part of the larger flow of life.

Modern Application:

1. Work-Life Balance: Understanding when to stop working and prioritize rest and personal life.

2. Goal Setting: Setting realistic limits and knowing when you've achieved enough.

3. Stress Management: Recognizing when to step back from stressful situations to preserve mental health.

4. Consumption: Practicing moderation in eating, drinking, spending, and use of resources.

5. Creativity: Knowing when a project is complete and resisting the urge to over-polish or perfect.

6. Debate and Discussion: Understanding when further argument is unproductive and it's time to agree to disagree.

7. Personal Growth: Balancing the drive for self-improvement with self-acceptance.

8. Environmental Stewardship: Recognizing the limits of resource use and the importance of conservation.

Practical steps:

- Practicing mindfulness to become more aware of your limits and natural stopping points
- Setting clear boundaries in work and personal life, and sticking to them
- Regularly assessing your goals and being willing to adjust or let go when appropriate
- Incorporating regular breaks and rest periods into your daily routine
- Before adding something new to your life, considering what you might need to stop doing to maintain balance
- In conversations or conflicts, practicing the art of timely disengagement
- When working on projects, defining clear criteria for completion to avoid endless tweaking
- Observing natural cycles and rhythms, and aligning your activities with them when possible

Reflection Questions:

1. Recall a time when knowing when to stop led to a positive outcome in your life. What did this experience teach you?

2. In what areas of your life do you tend to overextend yourself or have trouble stopping?

3. How might embracing Zhi Zhi change your approach to work, relationships, or personal goals?

4. What fears or beliefs might be driving you to push beyond healthy limits in certain areas of your life?

5. How does the idea of "knowing when to stop" challenge or support your views on achievement and success?

6. Think of someone you know who seems to embody Zhi Zhi. How does this quality manifest in their life?

7. How could practicing Zhi Zhi enhance your overall wellbeing and alignment with the Tao?

Remember, Zhi Zhi is not about limiting yourself or avoiding challenges, but about finding the natural limits and rhythms that allow for sustainable, harmonious living. As you explore this concept, pay attention to the subtle signals in your body, mind, and environment that indicate when it's time to pause or cease action. Developing this sensitivity can lead to a more balanced, effective, and fulfilling way of living in alignment with the Tao.

Chapter 45: Being Beyond Hua (Superficialities)

Beneath the glitter and the shine,
> Lies truth that's yours and truth that's mine,
> Beyond Hua's veil, we come to see,
> The essence of reality.
> The sage looks past the surface show,
> To depths where wisdom's waters flow,
> For in the real, beyond facade,
> We touch the heart of Tao's great art.

Explanation:

Being Beyond Hua (◇), or superficialities, is a key concept in Taoist philosophy that encourages looking past surface appearances to understand the deeper reality of things. Hua refers to the ornate, the flashy, or the superficially attractive, which can often distract us from what's truly important or real.

While not directly quoted in the Tao Te Ching, this concept aligns closely with Lao Tzu's teachings on simplicity and essence. For instance, he writes:

"The five colors blind the eye.

The five tones deafen the ear.

The five flavors dull the taste."

This passage suggests that an overemphasis on sensory or superficial experiences can actually hinder our perception of deeper truths.

In Taoist thought, true wisdom comes from penetrating beyond appearances to understand the underlying essence of things. This doesn't mean completely rejecting the world of form and appearance, but rather developing the discernment to see through it to the more fundamental reality beneath.

The concept of being beyond Hua is closely related to the Taoist ideal of Pu, or the "uncarved block," which represents a state of simplicity and potential before being shaped by external influences or desires. By moving beyond superficialities, we return to a more authentic and potent state of being.

Modern Application:

1. Media Literacy: Developing the ability to see beyond marketing and propaganda to understand underlying messages and motivations.

2. Personal authenticity: Cultivating a genuine self-expression that isn't overly concerned with

impressing others or conforming to societal expectations.

3. Consumerism: Resisting the allure of unnecessary purchases based on superficial appeal.

4. Relationships: Building connections based on genuine understanding rather than surface-level attractions.

5. Career Development: Focusing on developing real skills and value rather than just polishing one's image or resume.

6. Education: Emphasizing deep understanding and practical wisdom over rote memorization or credentials.

7. Art and Creativity: Creating work that communicates genuine meaning rather than just appealing to popular tastes.

8. Spiritual Practice: Moving beyond ritualistic or dogmatic aspects of spirituality to connect with deeper truths.

Practical steps:

- Practicing mindfulness to become more aware of your reactions to surface appearances
- Regularly questioning your assumptions and first impressions
- Engaging in periods of "information fasting" to reduce exposure to superficial stimuli
- When making decisions, taking time to look beyond immediate appeal to consider deeper value
- In conversations, practicing deep listening to understand beyond words and appearances
- Simplifying your living space, removing unnecessary ornamentations
- Exploring meditation practices that cultivate awareness of formless reality
- Regularly reflecting on your values and whether your actions truly align with them

Reflection Questions:

1. In what areas of your life do you find yourself most influenced by superficialities?

2. Can you recall a time when looking beyond appearances led to a valuable insight or experience?

3. How might your relationships change if you consistently looked beyond surface-level interactions?

4. What fears or insecurities might be keeping you attached to certain superficial aspects of your life?

5. How does the idea of moving beyond Hua challenge or support your current goals and aspirations?

6. Think of someone you admire for their ability to see beyond superficialities. What can you learn from them?

7. How could embracing this principle enhance your understanding of yourself and the world

around you?

Remember, being beyond Hua isn't about rejecting all form or beauty, but about developing the wisdom to see through to the essence of things. As you explore this concept, try to cultivate a balance between appreciating the world of form and understanding the deeper realities it may conceal. This discernment can lead to a more authentic, meaningful, and Tao-aligned way of living.

Chapter 46: Being An (Peacefully)

In stillness of the quiet mind,
  A peace profound, we come to find,
  An's gentle touch, like morning dew,
  Reveals the Tao in me and you.
  The sage, in tranquil waters deep,
  Knows secrets that the heavens keep,
  For in the calm of inner space,
  We meet the Tao in warm embrace.

Explanation:

An (◇), often translated as "peace" or "tranquility," is a fundamental concept in Taoist philosophy. It represents a state of inner calm and harmony that arises from alignment with the Tao. This peace is not just the absence of conflict, but a positive state of being that reflects one's connection with the natural order of the universe.

While the term An is not explicitly used in the Tao Te Ching, the concept is central to many of Lao Tzu's teachings. For instance, he writes:

"Empty your mind of all thoughts.

Let your heart be at peace.

Watch the turmoil of beings,

but contemplate their return."

This passage illustrates the Taoist path to inner peace through mindfulness and alignment with natural cycles.

In Taoist thought, true peace is not dependent on external circumstances, but is an internal state that can be cultivated through practice and understanding. This inner tranquility allows one to navigate life's challenges with equanimity and to respond to situations with clarity and wisdom.

The concept of An is closely related to the Taoist ideal of wu wei, or non-action. When one is in a state of deep peace, actions arise naturally and effortlessly in harmony with the Tao, without the need for forced effort or striving.

Modern Application:

1. Stress Management: Cultivating inner peace as a buffer against life's stresses and challenges.

2. Conflict Resolution: Approaching disagreements from a place of inner calm, leading to more harmonious solutions.

3. Decision Making: Using a peaceful mind to make clearer, more balanced decisions.

4. Creativity: Accessing deeper levels of creativity and insight through a calm and open mental state.

5. Relationships: Bringing a sense of peace into interactions, creating more harmonious connections.

6. Health and Well-being: Recognizing the link between inner peace and physical health.

7. Leadership: Leading others from a place of inner tranquility, inspiring calm and confidence.

8. Environmental Awareness: Extending one's sense of peace to foster a more harmonious relationship with nature.

Practical steps:

- Practicing daily meditation or mindfulness to cultivate inner calm
- Creating a peaceful environment in your living and working spaces
- Learning and practicing deep breathing techniques for instant calm
- Regularly spending time in nature to absorb its natural tranquility
- Practicing acceptance of things you cannot change
- Engaging in activities that promote flow states, like art, music, or sports
- Before reacting to stressful situations, pausing to center yourself
- Cultivating gratitude to foster a sense of contentment and peace

Reflection Questions:

1. When do you feel most at peace in your life? What characterizes these moments?

2. How might cultivating more inner peace change your response to challenges in your life?

3. In what ways do you currently disturb your own peace? How could you address these?

4. How does the idea of peace as an active, cultivated state challenge or support your current understanding?

5. Think of someone you know who embodies An. How does their peace affect those around them?

6. How might your relationships change if you approached them from a consistently peaceful state?

7. What practices or changes could you implement to bring more An into your daily life?

Remember, being An is not about escaping from life's realities or suppressing emotions. It's about developing a deep, abiding sense of inner peace that allows you to engage with life more fully and harmoniously. As you explore this concept, pay attention to the moments of peace in your day, no matter how brief, and consider how you might expand these to create a more tranquil way of being.

Chapter 47: Being by Zi (Being)

In simply being, truth unfolds,
As Zi reveals what life upholds,
Not doing, striving, or pursuit,
But present in our deepest root.
The sage, in being's gentle art,
Discovers wisdom's beating heart,
For in the is-ness of each hour,
We touch the Tao's eternal power.

Explanation:

Zi (◈), often translated as "self" or "naturalness," represents in Taoist philosophy the concept of simply being, without pretense or effort. It's about existing in one's most authentic state, in harmony with the Tao. This idea of "being" is not passive, but a dynamic state of alignment with one's true nature and the nature of the universe.

While not directly quoted in the Tao Te Ching, the concept of Zi is implicit in many of Lao Tzu's teachings. For instance, he writes:

"To understand the limitation of things, desire them.

To possess things without limit, detach from them.

When there is no desire, all things are at peace."

This passage illustrates the Taoist ideal of being in a state of natural harmony, free from the distortions of excessive desire or striving.

In Taoist thought, true being (Zi) is effortless and spontaneous. It's about letting go of artificial constructs and returning to one's original nature. This state of being is not about achieving something, but about allowing oneself to be as one truly is, in accordance with the Tao.

The concept of Zi is closely related to the Taoist principle of wu wei, or non-action. Both emphasize a way of existing and acting that is in natural harmony with the flow of life, without forced effort or resistance.

Modern Application:

1. Authenticity: Cultivating genuine self-expression free from societal masks or expectations.

2. Mindfulness: Practicing present-moment awareness, fully experiencing each moment of being.

3. Self-acceptance: Embracing oneself as one is, without constant striving for improvement or change.

4. Stress Reduction: Letting go of the need to constantly "do" and finding peace in simply being.

5. Creativity: Allowing creative expression to flow naturally from one's authentic self.

6. Relationships: Being present and genuine in interactions, fostering deeper connections.

7. Career Fulfillment: Aligning work with one's true nature for greater satisfaction and effectiveness.

8. Spiritual Practice: Moving beyond ritualistic or goal-oriented spirituality to a state of simple being.

Practical steps:

- Practicing mindfulness meditation to cultivate present-moment awareness
- Engaging in activities that allow you to lose self-consciousness and simply be (e.g., flow states in art or sports)
- Regularly checking in with yourself: "Am I being true to myself in this moment?"
- Creating periods of unstructured time in your schedule for simply being
- Practicing saying "no" to commitments that don't align with your true self
- Engaging in self-reflection to distinguish between authentic desires and conditioned wants
- Spending time in nature, observing the effortless being of plants and animals
- Experimenting with letting go of control in small situations and allowing things to unfold naturally

Reflection Questions:

1. When do you feel most authentically yourself, simply being without effort or pretense?

2. How might embracing Zi change your approach to personal growth or achievement?

3. In what areas of your life do you find it most challenging to simply be, without doing or striving?

4. How does the idea of "being" as an active, dynamic state challenge or support your current understanding?

5. Think of someone who seems to embody the quality of Zi. How does their way of being affect those around them?

6. How might your relationships change if you approached them from a state of simply being, rather than doing or achieving?

7. What fears or beliefs might be preventing you from fully embracing your natural state of being?

Remember, cultivating Zi is not about becoming passive or disengaged from life. It's about finding a way of engaging with the world that is more natural, authentic, and in harmony with the Tao. As you explore this concept, pay attention to moments when you feel most naturally yourself, without effort or pretense. These can be guideposts as you learn to embody Zi more fully in your daily life.

Chapter 48: Being by Jian (Decreasing)

In letting go, we come to gain,
As Jian reveals life's refrain,
Not loss or lack, but freedom found,
In simplicity, we're unbound.
The sage, in shedding excess weight,
Discovers Tao's unburdened state,
For in reduction's gentle art,
We find the whole within each part.

Explanation:

Jian (◇), often translated as "decrease" or "reduction," is a fundamental concept in Taoist philosophy. It embodies the idea that true abundance and freedom often come through lessening rather than accumulation. This principle suggests that by reducing excess, we can return to a more essential and harmonious state of being.

In the Tao Te Ching, Lao Tzu directly addresses this concept:

"In the pursuit of learning, every day something is acquired.

In the pursuit of Tao, every day something is dropped.

Less and less is done

Until non-action is achieved.

When nothing is done, nothing is left undone."

This passage illustrates the Taoist view that spiritual growth often involves a process of unlearning and letting go, rather than constantly acquiring and adding.

The principle of Jian is closely related to the Taoist ideal of simplicity. By reducing complexity in our lives, thoughts, and actions, we can align ourselves more closely with the natural simplicity of the Tao. This doesn't mean living in deprivation, but rather discerning what is essential and letting go of what is superfluous.

In nature, we see examples of Jian in the way trees shed their leaves in autumn, or how rivers naturally remove obstacles to flow more smoothly. These natural processes of reduction and simplification inspire the Taoist approach to life.

Jian also relates to the concept of wu wei, or effortless action. By reducing unnecessary efforts and complications, we can act more effectively and in greater harmony with the Tao.

Modern Application:

1. Minimalism: Embracing a lifestyle of owning and consuming less to focus on what's truly important.

2. Time Management: Reducing commitments and activities to create more space and freedom in one's schedule.

3. Mental Clarity: Practicing meditation and mindfulness to reduce mental clutter and achieve greater focus.

4. Stress Reduction: Simplifying one's life to reduce sources of stress and anxiety.

5. Environmental Sustainability: Reducing consumption and waste to live more harmoniously with the environment.

6. Communication: Using fewer, more precise words to convey meaning more effectively.

7. Problem Solving: Simplifying complex issues to their core elements for clearer solutions.

8. Personal Growth: Letting go of limiting beliefs, habits, or relationships to allow for new growth.

Practical steps:

- Decluttering your physical space, keeping only what is necessary or brings joy
- Practicing a "digital detox" by reducing time spent on devices or social media
- Simplifying your diet by focusing on whole, unprocessed foods
- Regularly reviewing your commitments and letting go of those that don't align with your priorities
- Practicing saying "no" to new obligations or possessions that don't add true value to your life
- Engaging in mindfulness meditation to reduce mental chatter
- In problem-solving, asking "What can I remove?" rather than "What can I add?"
- Observing natural cycles of reduction in nature and contemplating how they apply to your life

Reflection Questions:

1. In what areas of your life do you feel overburdened or cluttered? How might reduction bring more peace or clarity?

2. Can you recall a time when letting go of something (a possession, a belief, a habit) led to a sense of freedom or growth?

3. What fears or beliefs might be preventing you from embracing reduction in certain areas of your life?

4. How might practicing Jian change your approach to success or personal development?

5. Think of someone you know who embodies the principle of Jian. How does their approach to life differ from the norm?

6. In what ways might reducing or simplifying enhance your relationships or work life?

7. How does the idea of growth through reduction challenge or support your current worldview?

Remember, practicing Jian is not about depriving yourself or living in austerity. It's about finding the right balance and focusing on what's truly essential. As you explore this concept, pay attention to the sense of lightness and freedom that can come from letting go. The process of reduction can open up space for new insights, experiences, and ways of being that are more aligned with the Tao.

Chapter 49: Being Beyond Pan (Judgment)

Beyond the scales of right and wrong,

    Where judgments cease and peace belongs,

    Pan's rigid bounds we learn to shed,

    To wisdom's deeper truths we're led.

    The sage, in seeing all as one,

    Knows judging's work is never done,

    For in acceptance's wide embrace,

    We find the Tao's enduring grace.

Explanation:

Being Beyond Pan (◈), or judgment, is a profound concept in Taoist philosophy that encourages us to move beyond rigid categorizations of good and bad, right and wrong. It suggests that true wisdom lies in transcending dualistic thinking and embracing a more holistic view of reality.

While not directly quoted in the Tao Te Ching, this concept is implicit in many of Lao Tzu's teachings. For instance, he writes:

"When people see some things as beautiful,

other things become ugly.

When people see some things as good,

other things become bad."

This passage illustrates how judgments create artificial divisions and distort our perception of reality.

In Taoist thought, moving beyond judgment doesn't mean abandoning discernment or ethical behavior. Rather, it's about developing a deeper understanding that recognizes the interconnectedness of all things and the relative nature of our categorizations. It's about seeing the larger picture beyond our immediate reactions and preferences.

This principle is closely related to the Taoist concept of yin and yang, which sees apparent opposites as complementary aspects of a greater whole. By moving beyond judgment, we can appreciate the dynamic interplay of all aspects of life, rather than rigidly categorizing them as good or bad.

Being beyond Pan also aligns with the Taoist ideal of wu wei, or non-action. When we suspend judgment, we can respond to situations more spontaneously and appropriately, without being constrained by preconceived notions of how things should be.

Modern Application:

1. Conflict Resolution: Approaching disagreements with an open mind, seeing beyond right and wrong to find mutually beneficial solutions.

2. Personal Growth: Developing self-acceptance and reducing self-criticism by moving beyond harsh self-judgment.

3. Diversity and Inclusion: Cultivating genuine appreciation for differences rather than judging based on personal or cultural biases.

4. Decision Making: Considering multiple perspectives and potential outcomes rather than making snap judgments.

5. Creativity: Opening up to new ideas and possibilities by suspending judgment in the creative process.

6. Relationships: Fostering deeper understanding and empathy by withholding judgment of others' actions or choices.

7. Stress Reduction: Letting go of judgments about how things "should be," reducing anxiety and frustration.

8. Spiritual Practice: Developing a more inclusive and compassionate spirituality that goes beyond dogmatic judgments.

Practical steps:

- Practicing mindfulness to observe your thoughts and judgments without attaching to them
- When you notice yourself judging, pause and try to see the situation from multiple perspectives
- Engaging in perspective-taking exercises to understand viewpoints different from your own
- Practicing loving-kindness meditation to cultivate non-judgmental acceptance of yourself and others
- In conflicts, focusing on understanding all sides rather than determining who is right or wrong
- Regularly challenging your own assumptions and biases
- Studying philosophy or science to understand the relative nature of many of our judgments
- Engaging in activities that put you in contact with diverse groups of people

Reflection Questions:

1. In what areas of your life do you tend to be most judgmental? How does this affect you and others?

2. Can you recall a time when suspending judgment led to a surprising insight or positive outcome?

3. How might your relationships change if you consistently practiced being beyond Pan?

4. What fears or insecurities might be driving your need to judge in certain situations?

5. How does the idea of moving beyond judgment challenge or support your sense of ethics or morality?

6. Think of someone you admire for their non-judgmental attitude. What can you learn from them?

7. How could embracing this principle enhance your understanding of yourself and the world around you?

Remember, being beyond Pan isn't about becoming amoral or indifferent. It's about developing a wider, more compassionate perspective that recognizes the complexity of life beyond simple categories of good and bad. As you explore this concept, try to notice moments when you can suspend judgment and see situations with fresh eyes. This practice can lead to greater wisdom, compassion, and alignment with the Tao.

Chapter 50: Being as Xian (Immortal)

Beyond the bounds of mortal fears,
    The Xian's wisdom bright appears,
    Not endless life in flesh and bone,
    But timeless truth in Tao's own tone.
    The sage, in touching deathless grace,
    Transcends the limits of time and space,
    For in the eternal's vast expanse,
    We join creation's ageless dance.

Explanation:

The concept of Xian (⬦), often translated as "immortal" or "transcendent being," is a significant idea in Taoist philosophy and Chinese culture. However, it's important to understand that in Taoism, the notion of immortality goes beyond mere physical longevity. It represents a state of spiritual transcendence and harmony with the Tao that surpasses the limitations of ordinary existence.

While the Tao Te Ching doesn't directly discuss Xian, the concept aligns with many of Lao Tzu's teachings about aligning with the eternal Tao. For instance, he writes:

"The Tao never dies. It is the deep source of all things."

This passage hints at the immortal, ever-present nature of the Tao, which the Xian seeks to embody. In Taoist thought, becoming a Xian isn't about achieving physical immortality, but about transcending the cycle of life and death by aligning oneself completely with the Tao. It's about reaching a state of being where one is no longer bound by the limitations of the individual ego or the physical world.

The concept of Xian is closely related to the Taoist practices of internal alchemy and meditation, which aim to cultivate and refine one's essential nature or spirit. Through these practices, it is believed that one can attain a state of union with the Tao that transcends ordinary existence. Being as Xian also involves embodying virtues such as non-attachment, spontaneity, and harmony with nature. The Xian is often portrayed as someone who has let go of worldly concerns and lives in accordance with the natural flow of the Tao.

Modern Application:

1. Perspective Shifting: Cultivating a broader, more timeless perspective on life's challenges and joys.

2. Fear Management: Addressing fears, particularly the fear of death, by connecting with

something greater than individual existence.

3. Purpose and Meaning: Finding a sense of purpose that transcends personal gain or temporary achievements.

4. Creativity: Tapping into a sense of timelessness to access deeper wells of creativity and inspiration.

5. Environmental Stewardship: Developing a long-term, even "immortal" perspective on our relationship with the environment.

6. Legacy Building: Considering how our actions and choices resonate beyond our individual lifespans.

7. Stress Reduction: Letting go of short-term worries by connecting with a more eternal perspective.

8. Spiritual Practice: Deepening spiritual practices to cultivate a sense of connection with the timeless.

Practical steps:

- Practicing meditation to cultivate awareness of the timeless present moment
- Engaging in contemplative practices that explore the nature of consciousness and existence
- Studying philosophical or spiritual texts that discuss concepts of eternity and transcendence
- Regularly spending time in nature to connect with cycles and rhythms larger than human life
- Practicing letting go of attachments to transient things
- Engaging in creative activities that induce a sense of timelessness or "flow"
- Reflecting on your life from the perspective of future generations or a much older self
- Cultivating virtues and actions that have lasting, positive impacts beyond your own life

Reflection Questions:

1. What does the concept of immortality mean to you beyond mere physical longevity?

2. How might embracing the perspective of a Xian change your approach to daily challenges and long-term goals?

3. In what ways do you already experience moments of transcendence or timelessness in your life?

4. How does the idea of spiritual immortality challenge or support your current beliefs about life and death?

5. What attachments or fears might be preventing you from experiencing a more transcendent state of being?

6. How could cultivating a Xian-like perspective enhance your relationships and interactions with others?

7. What practices or changes could you implement to bring more of the Xian quality into your daily life?

Remember, being as Xian is not about escaping life or seeking literal immortality. It's about living fully in the present while maintaining a connection to the eternal, transcendent aspects of existence. As you explore this concept, pay attention to moments when you feel a sense of timelessness or connection to something greater than yourself. These experiences can be gateways to a deeper understanding of the Xian state and your relationship with the eternal Tao.

Chapter 51: Being by Xuan De (Hidden Virtue)

In silence deep, true virtue grows,
    As Xuan De's gentle wisdom flows,
    Not seeking praise or worldly fame,
    But nurturing Tao's hidden flame.
    The sage, in quiet deeds of grace,
    Reveals the Tao in every place,
    For in the unseen and unsung,
    The heart of virtue's song is strung.

Explanation:

Xuan De (◇◇), often translated as "profound virtue" or "hidden virtue," is a key concept in Taoist philosophy. It refers to a kind of virtue or power that operates subtly and without seeking recognition. This is not virtue in the conventional moral sense, but a deep alignment with the Tao that naturally expresses itself in harmonious action.

Lao Tzu speaks of this concept in the Tao Te Ching:

"The highest virtue is not virtuous, and so has virtue.

The lowest virtue never strays from virtue, and so is without virtue."

This paradoxical statement suggests that true virtue (Xuan De) operates naturally and spontaneously, without conscious effort or desire for recognition.

In Taoist thought, Xuan De is closely related to the concept of wu wei, or non-action. It's about allowing one's actions to arise naturally from one's alignment with the Tao, rather than from a desire to be seen as good or virtuous. This hidden virtue is considered more powerful and authentic than ostentatious displays of morality.

The "hidden" aspect of Xuan De is significant. It suggests that the most profound virtue often operates behind the scenes, influencing things in subtle ways that may not be immediately apparent. Like the Tao itself, Xuan De works in mysterious ways, nourishing and harmonizing without drawing attention to itself.

Cultivating Xuan De involves developing one's inner nature and allowing it to express itself spontaneously and appropriately in each situation. It's about being rather than doing, allowing one's innate virtue to manifest naturally rather than striving to be virtuous.

Modern Application:

1. Leadership: Leading by example and influence rather than through overt control or

manipulation.

2. Parenting: Nurturing children through one's own embodiment of values rather than through preaching or punishment.

3. Environmental Stewardship: Taking actions to benefit the environment without seeking recognition or reward.

4. Community Service: Engaging in acts of service motivated by genuine care rather than desire for acclaim.

5. Personal Growth: Focusing on inner development rather than outward appearances of success or virtue.

6. Conflict Resolution: Influencing situations positively through one's presence and attitude rather than through force or argument.

7. Creativity: Allowing creative work to arise naturally from one's inner state rather than forcing it for recognition.

8. Relationships: Cultivating genuine care and support that doesn't demand acknowledgment or reciprocation.

Practical steps:

- Practicing mindfulness to become more aware of your motivations for "virtuous" actions
- Engaging in anonymous acts of kindness or service
- Cultivating inner qualities like compassion, patience, and equanimity through meditation or reflection
- When doing good deeds, focus on the action itself rather than potential recognition or rewards
- Regularly reflecting on how your actions align with your inner values
- Practicing listening and observation more than speaking or acting
- In leadership or influential roles, focus on setting a good example rather than giving orders
- Studying nature to observe how it nurtures and sustains without seeking credit

Reflection Questions:

1. Can you recall a time when you acted virtuously without any expectation of recognition? How did it feel?

2. In what ways might you be seeking validation or recognition for your "good" actions?

3. How might embracing Xuan De change your approach to personal growth or success?

4. What hidden virtues do you recognize in others that inspire you?

5. How could cultivating Xuan De enhance your relationships or work life?

6. What fears or insecurities might be preventing you from embracing hidden virtue more fully?

7. How does the concept of Xuan De challenge or support your current understanding of ethics and morality?

Remember, cultivating Xuan De is not about suppressing your good deeds or becoming invisible. It's about allowing virtue to flow naturally from your alignment with the Tao, without attachment to recognition or results. As you explore this concept, pay attention to moments when you act from a place of spontaneous virtue, without calculation or desire for reward. These can be glimpses of Xuan De in action, guiding you towards a more profound and effortless expression of virtue in your life.

Chapter 52: Being by Gui Mu (Returning to the Mother)

In life's vast journey, far and wide,
    We find our way back to our side,
    Gui Mu, return to source divine,
    Where Tao and self do intertwine.
    The sage, in wisdom's gentle hold,
    Sees new beginnings in the old,
    For in return to primal womb,
    We find the Tao in fullest bloom.

Explanation:

Gui Mu (◇◇), which translates to "returning to the mother," is a profound concept in Taoist philosophy. It represents the idea of returning to one's origin, to the source of all being, which is often symbolized as the "mother" – the Tao itself. This concept embodies the cyclical nature of existence and the importance of reconnecting with our fundamental essence.

Lao Tzu addresses this concept in the Tao Te Ching:

"Returning to the source is stillness, which is the way of nature.

The way of nature is unchanging.

Knowing constancy is insight."

This passage highlights the Taoist belief that returning to our source brings us into alignment with the fundamental nature of the universe. In Taoist thought, "returning to the mother" is not just a philosophical idea, but a practical path of cultivation. It involves turning our attention inward, quieting the mind, and reconnecting with the primordial state of being that exists before thoughts, emotions, and individual identity arise.

This concept is closely related to the Taoist practices of meditation and inner alchemy, which aim to reverse the process of differentiation and return to a state of primordial unity with the Tao. It's about undoing the separateness that comes with individual existence and remembering our fundamental connection to all things. "Returning to the mother" also implies a kind of spiritual rebirth. By reconnecting with our source, we can renew ourselves, gain fresh perspective, and approach life with the openness and potential of a newborn.

Modern Application:

1. Stress Relief: Practicing techniques that help us return to a calm, centered state amidst life's chaos.

2. Creativity: Tapping into the source of inspiration by quieting the mind and connecting with our deeper self.

3. Problem Solving: Approaching challenges from a fresh perspective by returning to a state of open potential.

4. Personal Growth: Periodically "resetting" our patterns and habits by reconnecting with our core essence.

5. Relationships: Remembering our fundamental connection to others, fostering empathy and compassion.

6. Environmental Awareness: Recognizing our inseparability from nature, encouraging more harmonious interactions with the environment.

7. Spiritual Practice: Deepening meditation or contemplative practices that facilitate a return to our spiritual source.

8. Life Transitions: Navigating major life changes by viewing them as opportunities for renewal and return to essence.

Practical steps:

- Practicing meditation techniques that focus on returning to the breath or a state of pure awareness
- Engaging in regular periods of silence or solitude to facilitate inner connection
- Studying and practicing Taoist or other forms of meditation that emphasize returning to the source
- Spending time in nature, particularly in places that evoke a sense of primordial connection
- Reflecting on your life journey, recognizing cycles of departure and return
- Practicing letting go of acquired identities and roles to touch your essential nature
- Engaging in creative activities that allow you to enter a state of flow or timelessness
- Before making decisions, taking time to center yourself and connect with your deeper wisdom

Reflection Questions:

1. When do you feel most connected to your essential nature or "source"?

2. How might regularly "returning to the mother" change your approach to daily challenges and long-term goals?

3. What practices or experiences help you feel renewed or "reborn"?

4. How does the idea of returning to a primordial state challenge or support your sense of identity?

5. In what areas of your life do you feel most disconnected from your essence? How might you

reconnect?

6. How could embracing the concept of Gui Mu enhance your relationships or work life?

7. What fears or attachments might be preventing you from more fully "returning to the mother"?

Remember, "returning to the mother" is not about escaping life or regressing to an infantile state. It's about regularly reconnecting with our deepest essence to live more authentically and in greater harmony with the Tao. As you explore this concept, pay attention to moments when you feel a sense of returning to your core self or connecting with something greater. These experiences can guide you towards a deeper understanding of Gui Mu and its potential to enrich your life.

Chapter 53: Being Yi (Honorably)

In honor's path, we find our way,
    As Yi guides us through night and day,
    Not rigid rules or vain display,
    But inner truth in all we say.
    The sage, in dignity's embrace,
    Moves through the world with timeless grace,
    For in the noble heart's deep core,
    We touch the Tao forevermore.

Explanation:

Yi (⬦), often translated as "righteousness" or "honor," is a fundamental concept in Chinese philosophy, including Taoism. However, the Taoist understanding of Yi goes beyond conventional notions of morality or social propriety. It represents a deep, innate sense of what is right and fitting, arising from one's alignment with the Tao rather than from external rules or societal expectations.

While the Tao Te Ching doesn't explicitly use the term Yi, the concept is implicit in many of Lao Tzu's teachings about virtue and right action. For instance, he writes:

"The Master doesn't try to be powerful;

thus he is truly powerful.

The ordinary man keeps reaching for power;

thus he never has enough."

This passage illustrates the Taoist view that true honor and righteousness come from inner cultivation rather than external pursuits.

In Taoist thought, Yi is not about adhering to a fixed code of conduct, but about developing the wisdom to respond appropriately to each unique situation. It's a kind of ethical intuition that arises naturally when one is in harmony with the Tao. This honor is characterized by integrity, authenticity, and a deep respect for the natural order of things.

The concept of Yi is closely related to the Taoist ideal of wu wei, or effortless action. When one embodies true honor, right action flows spontaneously without the need for forced effort or deliberation. It's about being in such alignment with the Tao that one naturally does what is right and appropriate in each moment.

Yi also involves a sense of dignity and self-respect that doesn't depend on external validation. The sage who embodies Yi is honorable not because others recognize them as such, but because they are true to their own nature and to the Tao.

Modern Application:

1. Ethical Decision Making: Developing an inner moral compass that guides decisions beyond rigid rules.

2. Leadership: Leading with integrity and authenticity rather than through authority or manipulation.

3. Personal Relationships: Cultivating honesty and trustworthiness in all interactions.

4. Professional Conduct: Maintaining ethical standards not out of obligation, but from a place of inner conviction.

5. Self-Respect: Developing a sense of dignity and worth that isn't dependent on others' opinions.

6. Conflict Resolution: Approaching disagreements with a focus on what is right rather than who is right.

7. Social Responsibility: Acting for the greater good out of a sense of inner righteousness rather than external pressure.

8. Personal Growth: Striving for self-improvement driven by internal values rather than societal expectations.

Practical steps:

- Regularly reflecting on your core values and how they align with your actions
- Practicing mindfulness to become more aware of your motivations and the consequences of your actions
- When faced with ethical dilemmas, taking time to center yourself and listen to your inner wisdom
- Studying philosophical or spiritual texts that discuss ethics and honor from various perspectives
- Engaging in acts of integrity even when no one is watching or would know
- Practicing speaking your truth diplomatically but firmly, even when it's challenging
- Regularly assessing your actions: "Am I doing this because it's right, or for some other reason?"
- Cultivating relationships with people who embody honor and integrity

Reflection Questions:

1. What does being honorable mean to you personally, beyond societal definitions?

2. Can you recall a time when you acted with true honor, even at a personal cost? How did it feel?

3. In what areas of your life do you find it most challenging to maintain your integrity?

4. How might embracing Yi change your approach to difficult decisions or conflicts?

5. What fears or external pressures might be preventing you from fully embodying your sense of honor?

6. How could cultivating a deeper sense of Yi enhance your relationships and interactions with others?

7. Think of someone you consider truly honorable. What qualities do they embody that you admire?

Remember, being Yi is not about rigid morality or self-righteousness. It's about cultivating an inner sense of honor that naturally expresses itself in right action. As you explore this concept, pay attention to moments when you feel a deep, intuitive sense of what is right and fitting. These can be glimpses of Yi guiding you towards a more honorable and Tao-aligned way of being in the world.

Chapter 54: Being as If Wu Wei (Your Life Makes a Difference)

In effortless grace, we find our might,
    As if Wu Wei, we touch the light,
    Not idle drift or forced control,
    But active peace in heart and soul.
    The sage, in doing without do,
    Creates a world forever new,
    For in the dance of letting be,
    We shape the future's destiny.

Explanation:

The concept of "Being as If Wu Wei" (◇◇) combines the Taoist principle of non-action with the understanding that our very existence inherently makes a difference in the world. This paradoxical idea suggests that we can have the most profound impact when we act without forcing or striving, allowing our actions to arise naturally from our alignment with the Tao.

Lao Tzu speaks of Wu Wei in the Tao Te Ching:

"The Master does nothing, yet he leaves nothing undone.

The ordinary man is always doing things, yet many more are left to be done."

This passage illustrates the power of Wu Wei - the ability to accomplish much without forced effort.

In Taoist philosophy, Wu Wei doesn't mean literal inaction, but rather action that is in such perfect harmony with the natural flow of the Tao that it seems effortless. It's about aligning oneself so completely with the natural order that one's actions become an organic part of the universal process.

The addition of "as if" and the idea that "your life makes a difference" brings a nuanced perspective to this concept. It suggests that while we embody the principle of Wu Wei, we also recognize the inherent significance of our existence and actions. Every moment, every choice, every breath is part of the cosmic dance and contributes to the unfolding of reality.

This principle encourages us to trust in the natural unfolding of events while also recognizing our role in shaping that unfolding. It's about finding the balance between active engagement and allowing things to take their course.

Modern Application:

1. Leadership: Guiding others through inspiration and example rather than through force or

control.

2. Creativity: Allowing ideas and inspiration to flow naturally rather than forcing creativity.

3. Problem Solving: Approaching challenges with a relaxed, open mind, allowing solutions to emerge organically.

4. Relationships: Interacting with others in a way that is genuine and unforced, yet deeply impactful.

5. Personal Growth: Trusting in one's natural development while also actively engaging in self-cultivation.

6. Environmental Stewardship: Recognizing that our very existence affects the environment and acting in harmony with natural processes.

7. Social Change: Working towards positive change through alignment with natural social evolution rather than forceful imposition.

8. Stress Management: Accomplishing tasks with a sense of ease and flow rather than strain and struggle.

Practical steps:

- Practicing mindfulness to become more aware of the natural flow of events and your place within them
- Regularly reflecting on how your actions, even small ones, ripple out to affect the world
- When faced with challenges, taking a step back to observe before acting
- Cultivating trust in your innate abilities and intuitions
- Practicing letting go of the need to control outcomes while still engaging fully in the process
- Observing nature to learn about effortless action and natural cycles
- In your work or creative pursuits, allowing periods of "non-doing" to let ideas and solutions emerge
- Regularly asking yourself, "How can I accomplish this with less force and more alignment?"

Reflection Questions:

1. Can you recall a time when you effortlessly made a significant difference? What characterized this experience?

2. How might embracing "being as if Wu Wei" change your approach to your goals and ambitions?

3. In what areas of your life do you tend to force things? How could you bring more Wu Wei into these areas?

4. How does the idea that your life inherently makes a difference challenge or support your current worldview?

5. What fears or beliefs might be preventing you from trusting in Wu Wei more fully?

6. How could embodying this principle enhance your relationships or work life?

7. Think of someone who seems to effortlessly make a positive impact. What can you learn from their approach?

Remember, "Being as If Wu Wei" is not about becoming passive or abdicating responsibility. It's about recognizing that your very existence is significant and impactful, while also aligning yourself with the natural flow of the Tao to act with grace and effectiveness. As you explore this concept, pay attention to moments when your actions feel both effortless and deeply meaningful. These can be guideposts as you learn to navigate life with the paradoxical power of Wu Wei.

Chapter 55: Being by Fang Xia (Letting Go)

In open hands, true freedom lies,
    As Fang Xia teaches us to rise,
    Not loss or lack, but space to grow,
    In letting go, we come to know.
    The sage, unburdened, light and free,
    Embraces life's grand mystery,
    For in release of all we cling,
    We touch the Tao in everything.

Explanation:

Fang Xia (◇◇), which translates to "letting go" or "putting down," is a fundamental concept in Taoist philosophy. It represents the practice of releasing attachments, preconceptions, and desires that bind us and prevent us from flowing with the Tao. This principle is not about renunciation or denial, but about freeing ourselves from the mental and emotional burdens that cloud our perception and hinder our natural alignment with the way of things.

While the Tao Te Ching doesn't use the exact term Fang Xia, the concept is implicit in many of Lao Tzu's teachings. For instance, he writes:

"In the pursuit of knowledge, every day something is added.

In the practice of the Tao, every day something is dropped."

This passage illustrates the Taoist emphasis on simplification and letting go as a path to wisdom.

In Taoist thought, letting go is not a one-time action but a continuous practice. It involves constantly releasing our grip on fixed ideas, expectations, and attachments that arise in our daily lives. This doesn't mean becoming detached or indifferent, but rather developing a kind of responsive flexibility that allows us to move with the changes of life without being bound by our own mental constructs.

Fang Xia is closely related to the Taoist concept of wu wei, or non-action. By letting go of our need to control and manipulate situations, we can act more spontaneously and effectively in harmony with the natural flow of events.

The practice of letting go also connects to the Taoist understanding of the cyclical nature of existence. By willingly releasing what is no longer serving us, we create space for new growth and transformation, aligning ourselves with the natural processes of change and renewal.

Modern Application:

1. Stress Reduction: Letting go of worries, regrets, and anxieties that create mental and emotional tension.

2. Adaptability: Releasing rigid expectations to become more flexible in the face of change.

3. Relationships: Letting go of past hurts, unrealistic expectations, or the need to control others.

4. Personal Growth: Releasing limiting beliefs and self-concepts that hinder our development.

5. Creativity: Letting go of preconceived notions to allow new ideas and inspirations to emerge.

6. Decision Making: Releasing attachment to outcomes to make clearer, more balanced choices.

7. Time Management: Letting go of non-essential tasks and commitments to focus on what truly matters.

8. Spiritual Practice: Releasing ego-attachments to deepen one's connection with the Tao.

Practical steps:

- Practicing mindfulness meditation to observe thoughts and emotions without clinging to them
- Regularly decluttering physical spaces as a tangible practice of letting go
- When facing difficulties, asking "What can I let go of in this situation?"
- Engaging in release rituals, such as writing down what you want to let go of and burning the paper
- Practicing acceptance of things you cannot change
- Regularly reviewing your commitments and letting go of those that no longer serve you
- Exploring body-based practices like yoga or qigong that involve physical releasing
- Before bed each night, consciously "putting down" the events of the day

Reflection Questions:

1. What are you currently holding onto that might be holding you back?

2. Can you recall a time when letting go led to unexpected positive outcomes?

3. How might your life change if you practiced Fang Xia more consistently?

4. What fears or beliefs make it challenging for you to let go in certain areas of your life?

5. How does the idea of constant letting go challenge or support your goals and aspirations?

6. Think of someone who embodies the quality of Fang Xia. How does their approach to life differ from the norm?

7. In what ways could letting go enhance your relationships or work life?

Remember, Fang Xia is not about becoming detached or apathetic. It's about creating space in our lives and in our minds for greater wisdom, peace, and alignment with the Tao. As you explore this concept, pay attention to the sense of lightness and freedom that can come from letting go. The practice of Fang Xia can open up new possibilities and allow for a more flowing, harmonious way of being in the world.

Chapter 56: Being by Ji Mo (Silent Knowing)

In silence deep, true wisdom grows,
    As Ji Mo's quiet insight flows,
    Not words or thoughts, but knowing's light,
    Illuminates the darkest night.
    The sage, in stillness, understands,
    The whispered truths of distant lands,
    For in the hush of inner space,
    We touch the Tao's eternal grace.

Explanation:

Ji Mo (◇◇), which can be translated as "silent knowing" or "quiet understanding," is a profound concept in Taoist philosophy. It represents a state of deep, intuitive wisdom that arises not from intellectual knowledge or verbal discourse, but from a place of inner stillness and direct perception.

While the term Ji Mo is not explicitly used in the Tao Te Ching, the concept is central to many of Lao Tzu's teachings. He writes:

"Those who know do not speak.

Those who speak do not know."

This famous passage highlights the Taoist emphasis on a wisdom that transcends words and concepts.

In Taoist thought, Ji Mo is not merely about being physically silent, but about cultivating an inner quietude that allows for a deeper, more direct understanding of reality. It's a state where the constant chatter of the mind subsides, allowing for a more profound connection with the Tao and the true nature of things.

This silent knowing is considered superior to intellectual knowledge because it's not limited by the constraints of language or conceptual thinking. It's a holistic, intuitive grasp of reality that comes from being in harmony with the Tao rather than from accumulating information or ideas.

Ji Mo is closely related to the Taoist practices of meditation and inner cultivation. Through these practices, one learns to quiet the mind and open oneself to a more direct, unmediated experience of reality. This state of silent knowing is seen as the source of true wisdom and effective action.

The concept also relates to the Taoist ideal of wu wei, or non-action. From a state of silent knowing, one can respond to situations spontaneously and appropriately, without the need for excessive deliberation or forced effort.

Modern Application:

1. Decision Making: Cultivating intuitive wisdom to complement analytical thinking in making choices.

2. Creativity: Accessing deeper wells of inspiration by quieting the mind and listening to inner promptings.

3. Relationships: Developing the ability to understand others beyond words, enhancing empathy and connection.

4. Problem Solving: Allowing solutions to emerge from a place of inner quiet rather than constant mental activity.

5. Self-Understanding: Gaining deeper insights into oneself through practices that cultivate inner silence.

6. Stress Reduction: Finding peace and clarity by stepping back from mental noise and connecting with inner stillness.

7. Leadership: Developing the capacity for deep listening and intuitive understanding in guiding others.

8. Spiritual Growth: Deepening one's spiritual practice through cultivation of silent, direct perception.

Practical steps:

- Practicing silent meditation, focusing on cultivating inner quietude
- Engaging in regular periods of solitude and silence
- When faced with problems, taking time for quiet reflection before acting
- Practicing mindful listening in conversations, attuning to what's beyond the words
- Exploring contemplative practices like Zen meditation or Taoist inner alchemy
- Regularly unplugging from technology to reduce mental noise
- Before making decisions, taking time to tune into your intuitive sense
- Cultivating moments of stillness throughout the day, even in the midst of activity

Reflection Questions:

1. When have you experienced a moment of deep, wordless understanding? What characterized this experience?

2. How might cultivating Ji Mo change your approach to decision-making or problem-solving?

3. In what areas of your life do you tend to rely too heavily on verbal or intellectual understanding?

4. How does the idea of wisdom beyond words challenge or support your current approach to learning and growth?

5. What obstacles do you face in cultivating more inner silence in your daily life?

6. How could embracing Ji Mo enhance your relationships or work life?

7. Think of a time when you "knew" something without being able to explain how. What can this teach you about silent knowing?

Remember, Ji Mo is not about suppressing thought or becoming unresponsive. It's about accessing a deeper level of wisdom and perception that goes beyond conceptual thinking. As you explore this concept, pay attention to moments of clarity or understanding that arise from stillness rather than active thought. These can be glimpses of Ji Mo, guiding you towards a more profound and intuitive way of engaging with life and the Tao.

Chapter 57: Being Without Jun (Authoritarianism)

In freedom's dance, true power lies,
    As life without Jun's chains arise,
    Not chaos wild or rule supreme,
    But harmony in Tao's regime.
    The sage, in leading, sets all free,
    To find their own authority,
    For in the space where control ends,
    The Tao its boundless grace extends.

Explanation:

Being Without Jun (◇), or authoritarianism, is a crucial concept in Taoist philosophy that advocates for a way of governing and living that is free from coercive power and rigid control. In this context, Jun represents not just political authoritarianism, but any form of domineering force that imposes its will on others or on natural processes.

Lao Tzu addresses this concept in the Tao Te Ching:

"Govern a great nation as you would cook a small fish; do not overdo it."

This passage illustrates the Taoist preference for minimal intervention and the trust in natural processes.

In Taoist thought, being without Jun doesn't mean descending into chaos or abandoning all forms of organization. Rather, it suggests a more organic, responsive way of managing affairs that aligns with the natural flow of the Tao. It's about creating conditions where things can self-organize and flourish according to their own nature, rather than imposing external control.

This principle applies not just to governance, but to all aspects of life. In personal relationships, work environments, and even in our relationship with ourselves, the Taoist ideal is to minimize forceful control and instead cultivate an environment of mutual respect, natural harmony, and spontaneous order.

Being without Jun is closely related to the Taoist concept of wu wei, or non-action. It suggests that the most effective way to lead or manage is often through subtle influence and by setting up the right conditions, rather than through direct force or micromanagement.

This approach also recognizes the wisdom inherent in natural systems and in individuals. By refraining from excessive control, we allow this innate wisdom to express itself and find its own solutions.

Modern Application:

1. Leadership: Developing a more facilitative, empowering style of leadership that trusts in team members' capabilities.

2. Parenting: Adopting a parenting approach that guides rather than controls, allowing children to develop their own strengths and autonomy.

3. Education: Creating learning environments that foster self-directed learning and intrinsic motivation.

4. Organizational Management: Implementing more flexible, decentralized organizational structures that allow for greater employee autonomy and innovation.

5. Personal Development: Letting go of rigid self-control and trusting more in one's natural inclinations and rhythms.

6. Environmental Stewardship: Working with natural processes rather than trying to dominate or overly manage ecosystems.

7. Conflict Resolution: Approaching disputes with a focus on finding mutually beneficial solutions rather than imposing one's will.

8. Community Organization: Fostering community initiatives that arise organically from local needs and strengths rather than top-down planning.

Practical steps:

- Practicing delegation and trust in professional or personal leadership roles
- When faced with problems, resisting the urge to immediately take control and instead observing how situations might naturally resolve
- In relationships, practicing active listening and seeking to understand rather than to direct or change others
- Experimenting with more democratic or consensual decision-making processes in groups
- Regularly reflecting on areas in your life where you might be exerting unnecessary control
- Studying natural ecosystems to understand how order can arise without centralized control
- In personal habits or goals, focusing on setting up supportive environments rather than relying solely on willpower
- Practicing letting go of the need to always be in charge or have things done your way

Reflection Questions:

1. In what areas of your life do you tend to exert the most control? How might loosening this control change things?

2. Can you recall a situation where letting go of control led to a better outcome than you could have planned?

3. How does the idea of being without Jun challenge or support your current leadership style or approach to responsibility?

4. What fears or beliefs might be driving a need for control in certain aspects of your life?

5. How might your relationships or work environment change if you embraced a less authoritarian approach?

6. Think of a time when you experienced the benefits of a non-authoritarian environment. What made this experience positive?

7. How could you apply the principle of being without Jun to a current challenge or goal in your life?

Remember, being without Jun is not about abdicating responsibility or embracing disorder. It's about finding a more natural, harmonious way of managing affairs that aligns with the Tao. As you explore this concept, pay attention to instances where letting go of control actually leads to better outcomes. These can be opportunities to deepen your trust in the natural unfolding of events and to cultivate a more Tao-aligned approach to leadership and life.

Chapter 58: Being Untroubled by Ji (Good or Bad Fortune)

Beyond the dance of loss and gain,
> The sage finds peace in joy and pain,
> Untroubled by Ji's ebb and flow,
> In Tao's embrace, all fortunes grow.
> Not bound by luck or circumstance,
> We learn to lead life's sacred dance,
> For in acceptance, deep and true,
> We find the Tao in all we do.

Explanation:

Being untroubled by Ji (⬦), which can refer to both good and bad fortune, is a profound concept in Taoist philosophy. It represents a state of equanimity and non-attachment to the ever-changing circumstances of life, whether they appear favorable or unfavorable.

While the Tao Te Ching doesn't explicitly use the term Ji, Lao Tzu addresses this concept in various passages. For instance:

"Accept disgrace willingly.

Accept misfortune as the human condition.

What do you mean by 'Accept disgrace willingly'?

Accept being unimportant.

Do not be concerned with loss or gain.

This is called 'accepting disgrace willingly.'"

This passage illustrates the Taoist ideal of maintaining inner peace regardless of external circumstances.

In Taoist thought, being untroubled by Ji doesn't mean becoming indifferent or apathetic. Rather, it's about developing a deeper understanding of the cyclical nature of existence and the interconnectedness of all things. From this perspective, what appears as good fortune or bad fortune are simply different manifestations of the same underlying reality.

This principle encourages us to look beyond immediate appearances and to trust in the larger process of the Tao. It suggests that what we perceive as misfortune may contain hidden blessings, and what seems like good luck may bring unexpected challenges.

Being untroubled by Ji is closely related to the Taoist concept of wu wei, or non-action. By not attaching too strongly to outcomes or reacting dramatically to changing circumstances, we can maintain our center and respond more effectively to life's ups and downs.

This approach also fosters resilience and adaptability. When we're not overly elated by success or devastated by failure, we can navigate life's changes with greater ease and wisdom.

Modern Application:

1. Stress Management: Developing emotional resilience in the face of life's ups and downs.

2. Decision Making: Making choices based on wisdom and principles rather than fear of bad outcomes or pursuit of good fortune.

3. Career Development: Maintaining motivation and effort regardless of immediate results or recognition.

4. Relationships: Cultivating steadiness in relationships, not being swayed by temporary conflicts or infatuations.

5. Financial Planning: Approaching finances with a long-term perspective, not being overly reactive to market fluctuations.

6. Personal Growth: Viewing challenges as opportunities for learning and development rather than as misfortunes.

7. Mental Health: Reducing anxiety and depression by lessening the emotional impact of external events.

8. Leadership: Providing stable guidance and inspiration, regardless of immediate circumstances.

Practical steps:

- Practicing mindfulness to observe your reactions to good and bad news without getting caught up in them
- Keeping a "fortune journal" where you reflect on how apparent good or bad fortune has played out in your life over time
- When facing setbacks, habitually asking "What opportunity might this present?"
- In times of success, practicing humility and considering potential challenges that may arise
- Regularly reminding yourself of the impermanent nature of all circumstances
- Studying philosophy or spirituality to deepen your understanding of life's cyclic nature
- Engaging in practices like meditation or tai chi that cultivate inner stability
- Developing a long-term perspective in your goals and plans, not being swayed by short-term fluctuations

Reflection Questions:

1. Recall a time when apparent misfortune led to unexpected positive outcomes. What did this teach you?

2. How might your life change if you were truly untroubled by good or bad fortune?

3. In what areas of your life do you tend to be most affected by the swings of fortune?

4. How does the idea of being untroubled by Ji challenge or support your current approach to success and failure?

5. What fears or attachments might be preventing you from maintaining equanimity in the face of changing circumstances?

6. Think of someone who embodies this quality of being untroubled by fortune. How does their approach to life differ from the norm?

7. How could embracing this principle enhance your relationships or work life?

Remember, being untroubled by Ji is not about becoming passive or indifferent to life's experiences. It's about developing a deeper, more stable center from which to engage with life's ever-changing circumstances. As you explore this concept, pay attention to how your perception of events shifts when you view them through this lens of equanimity. This practice can lead to a more peaceful, wise, and Tao-aligned way of navigating life's journey.

Chapter 59: Being by Jie Yue (Thrift and Moderation)

In simplicity's embrace we find,
    The wealth that truly frees the mind,
    Jie Yue's path of measured grace,
    Reveals the Tao in every place.
    The sage, content with what's at hand,
    Finds richness in both sea and land,
    For in the art of living light,
    We touch the Tao, both day and night.

Explanation:

Jie Yue (◇◇), which translates to "thrift" or "moderation," is a key principle in Taoist philosophy that emphasizes the value of living simply and avoiding excess. This concept goes beyond mere financial frugality; it encompasses a holistic approach to life that values sufficiency over abundance, quality over quantity, and mindful use of resources.

Lao Tzu addresses this concept in the Tao Te Ching:
"He who knows he has enough is rich.
Perseverance is a sign of willpower.
He who stays where he is endures.
To die but not to perish is to be eternally present."

This passage highlights the Taoist view that true wealth comes from contentment and moderation, not from excessive accumulation.

In Taoist thought, Jie Yue is not about deprivation or austerity, but about finding the right balance and recognizing when enough is enough. It's about using resources wisely and appreciating what we have, rather than constantly seeking more. This principle applies not just to material possessions, but to all aspects of life – our time, energy, relationships, and even our thoughts and emotions.

The practice of Jie Yue is seen as a way of aligning ourselves with the natural rhythms of the Tao. In nature, we see examples of efficiency and balance – nothing is wasted, and everything exists in the right proportion. By embodying this principle, we can live more harmoniously with ourselves, others, and the environment.

Jie Yue is closely related to the Taoist concept of wu wei, or effortless action. By living moderately and avoiding excess, we reduce the complications and burdens in our lives, allowing for a more natural and effortless way of being.

This principle also fosters a sense of gratitude and contentment. When we practice moderation, we learn to appreciate what we have more fully, finding richness and satisfaction in simplicity.

Modern Application:

1. Financial Management: Adopting a mindful approach to spending and saving, focusing on needs rather than wants.

2. Consumption Habits: Practicing conscious consumption, considering the environmental and social impact of our choices.

3. Time Management: Balancing work, rest, and leisure, avoiding the extremes of overwork or idleness.

4. Diet and Nutrition: Eating moderately and mindfully, avoiding excess in both quantity and variety.

5. Environmental Stewardship: Reducing waste and using resources efficiently to minimize our ecological footprint.

6. Emotional Regulation: Cultivating emotional balance, avoiding extreme highs and lows.

7. Information Consumption: Practicing moderation in media and information intake to avoid overwhelm and maintain mental clarity.

8. Relationship Building: Fostering quality relationships rather than seeking a large quantity of superficial connections.

Practical steps:

- Conducting a "life audit" to identify areas of excess or waste in your daily life
- Implementing a budget that prioritizes needs and meaningful experiences over material accumulation
- Practicing the "one in, one out" rule for possessions to maintain balance
- Regularly decluttering your physical and digital spaces
- Experimenting with periods of voluntary simplicity or fasting (from food, media, shopping, etc.)
- Before making purchases, pausing to reflect on whether the item is truly needed
- Cultivating hobbies and interests that don't require significant material resources
- Practicing gratitude daily for what you already have

Reflection Questions:

1. In what areas of your life do you tend towards excess? How does this affect your overall well-being?

2. Can you recall a time when having less actually led to greater satisfaction or freedom? What

did this experience teach you?

3. How might embracing Jie Yue change your approach to success or personal fulfillment?

4. What fears or beliefs might be driving a need for excess in certain aspects of your life?

5. How could practicing moderation enhance your relationships or work life?

6. Think of someone you know who embodies the principle of Jie Yue. How does their lifestyle differ from the norm, and what can you learn from them?

7. In what ways might adopting a more moderate lifestyle contribute to your spiritual or personal growth?

Remember, Jie Yue is not about depriving yourself or living in austerity. It's about finding the sweet spot of sufficiency where you have what you need to live well without the burden of excess. As you explore this concept, pay attention to the sense of freedom and contentment that can come from simplifying and moderating various aspects of your life. The practice of Jie Yue can lead to a more balanced, sustainable, and Tao-aligned way of living.

Chapter 60: Being with Wu Jian (Immunity to Evil)

In virtue's light, no shadow falls,
  As Wu Jian's strength within us calls,
  Not battle fierce or shield of might,
  But inner glow that banish night.
  The sage, immune to darkness' sway,
  Walks unscathed through night and day,
  For in the heart aligned with Tao,
  No evil finds a place to grow.

Explanation:

Wu Jian (◇◇), which can be translated as "immunity to evil" or "invulnerability," is a profound concept in Taoist philosophy. It represents a state of being where one is so aligned with the Tao that they become impervious to negative influences or harmful energies. This is not a physical invulnerability, but a spiritual and moral resilience that comes from deep inner cultivation.

While the term Wu Jian is not explicitly used in the Tao Te Ching, the concept is implicit in many of Lao Tzu's teachings. For instance, he writes:

"The Master doesn't try to be powerful;

thus he is truly powerful.

The ordinary man keeps reaching for power;

thus he never has enough."

This passage illustrates the Taoist view that true power and invulnerability come from inner cultivation rather than external defenses.

In Taoist thought, Wu Jian is not about fighting against evil or creating impenetrable barriers. Instead, it's about cultivating such a strong alignment with the Tao that negative influences naturally find no purchase. It's like water flowing around a rock – the water (representing negative influences) doesn't fight the rock, but simply moves around it, leaving it untouched.

This concept is closely related to the Taoist ideal of De, or virtue. By cultivating inner virtue and harmony with the Tao, one naturally repels that which is not in alignment with these principles. It's not an active resistance, but a natural incompatibility.

Wu Jian also involves a kind of spiritual discernment. When one is deeply attuned to the Tao, they can naturally distinguish between what is aligned with it and what is not, allowing them to navigate life's challenges with wisdom and clarity.

This principle doesn't mean that one never faces difficulties or challenges. Rather, it suggests that when one is in harmony with the Tao, they can move through these challenges without being internally disturbed or corrupted by them.

Modern Application:

1. Emotional Resilience: Developing inner strength to remain unaffected by negative emotions or external stressors.

2. Ethical Integrity: Cultivating such strong personal values that unethical temptations naturally hold no appeal.

3. Mental Health: Building psychological resilience against anxiety, depression, and other mental health challenges.

4. Conflict Resolution: Approaching conflicts with a calm, centered presence that naturally diffuses tension.

5. Personal Boundaries: Establishing clear, strong boundaries without the need for confrontation or aggression.

6. Leadership: Leading with integrity and principle, naturally inspiring ethical behavior in others.

7. Digital Wellbeing: Developing discernment and resilience in the face of online negativity or manipulation.

8. Spiritual Growth: Cultivating a strong spiritual core that remains steady amidst life's ups and downs.

Practical steps:

- Practicing daily meditation or mindfulness to strengthen your connection with your inner self
- Regularly reflecting on and reinforcing your core values and principles
- Studying philosophical or spiritual texts that deepen your understanding of ethics and virtue
- Engaging in practices like qigong or tai chi that cultivate both inner and outer strength
- When faced with negativity, practicing non-reaction and observing without engagement
- Cultivating positive, supportive relationships that reinforce your values
- Regularly exposing yourself to uplifting, inspiring content that aligns with your ideals
- Practicing forgiveness and compassion to release the hold of past negative experiences

Reflection Questions:

1. Can you recall a time when you felt impervious to negative influences? What characterized this experience?

2. How might embracing Wu Jian change your approach to challenges or conflicts in your life?

3. In what areas do you feel most vulnerable to negative influences? How could you strengthen

your immunity in these areas?

4. How does the idea of invulnerability through alignment with the Tao challenge or support your current understanding of strength and protection?

5. What practices or habits in your life contribute to your sense of inner strength and immunity?

6. Think of someone who seems to embody Wu Jian. How do they navigate difficulties differently from others?

7. How could cultivating Wu Jian enhance your relationships or your role in your community?

Remember, Wu Jian is not about becoming hard or insensitive. It's about developing such a strong inner core and alignment with the Tao that you naturally remain unaffected by negative influences. As you explore this concept, pay attention to moments when you feel a sense of inner steadiness or natural resistance to negativity. These can be glimpses of Wu Jian, guiding you towards a more resilient and Tao-aligned way of being in the world.

Chapter 61: Being by Qu (Remaining Low)

In lowly places, wisdom flows,
    As Qu reveals what heaven knows,
    Not weakness, but the strength to yield,
    In humble depths, great power sealed.
    The sage, in bowing, rises high,
    Like valleys drawing waters nigh,
    For in the low and quiet way,
    We touch the Tao from day to day.

Explanation:

Qu (◈), which can be translated as "to bend," "to yield," or "to remain low," is a fundamental concept in Taoist philosophy. It embodies the idea that true strength and wisdom often come from humility, flexibility, and the willingness to take the lower position. This principle is not about subservience or weakness, but about understanding the power of yielding and the strength found in apparent lowliness.

Lao Tzu addresses this concept directly in the Tao Te Ching:

"The highest good is like water.

Water gives life to the ten thousand things and does not strive.

It flows in places men reject and so is like the Tao."

This passage illustrates the Taoist admiration for the qualities of water – its ability to nourish all things while always seeking the lowest places.

In Taoist thought, remaining low is not about diminishing oneself, but about aligning with the natural tendencies of the Tao. It's a recognition that in nature, things that are low and yielding often endure and thrive, while those that are rigid and lofty are more easily toppled or broken.

The concept of Qu is closely related to the Taoist principle of wu wei, or non-action. By remaining low and yielding, one can often achieve more than through forceful assertion or striving. It's about finding the path of least resistance and working with natural tendencies rather than against them.

This principle also embodies the Taoist appreciation for the feminine or yin aspects of nature. The low, the yielding, the receptive – these are seen as powerful and essential qualities, balancing and often overcoming the more obvious strength of the masculine or yang.

Qu also relates to the idea of returning to one's root or origin. By remaining low, we stay connected to our source and maintain a grounded, authentic presence in the world.

Modern Application:

1. Leadership: Practicing servant leadership, where influence comes from supporting and uplifting others rather than dominating.

2. Conflict Resolution: Approaching disagreements with a willingness to listen and understand rather than to overpower or win.

3. Personal Growth: Cultivating humility and openness to learning, recognizing that growth often comes from acknowledging what we don't know.

4. Problem Solving: Approaching challenges from different angles, including "lower" or less obvious perspectives.

5. Career Development: Building a strong foundation and mastering basics before seeking advancement or recognition.

6. Relationships: Fostering deeper connections by being willing to be vulnerable and to prioritize others' needs.

7. Stress Management: Letting go of the need to always be "on top" or in control, finding peace in acceptance and flexibility.

8. Environmental Stewardship: Recognizing the value of humble, often overlooked elements in ecosystems and society.

Practical steps:

- Practicing active listening in conversations, focusing on understanding rather than responding or asserting your view
- Regularly seeking feedback and being open to constructive criticism
- Engaging in service activities where you support others without recognition
- When faced with conflicts, trying to see the situation from the other person's perspective first
- Cultivating a beginner's mindset, approaching tasks and learning with openness and humility
- In your work or creative pursuits, focusing on the process and craft rather than on accolades or results
- Practicing yielding in physical activities like tai chi or yoga to embody the principle of Qu
- Regularly reflecting on your own limitations and areas for growth

Reflection Questions:

1. Can you recall a time when taking a "lower" position or yielding led to a positive outcome? What did this teach you?

2. How might embracing Qu change your approach to leadership or influence in your life?

3. In what areas of your life do you find it most challenging to "remain low"? What drives this difficulty?

4. How does the idea of strength through yielding challenge or support your current understanding of power and effectiveness?

5. Think of someone you know who embodies the quality of Qu. How does their approach to life differ from the norm?

6. How could practicing "remaining low" enhance your relationships or work life?

7. What fears or beliefs might be preventing you from embracing Qu more fully in certain situations?

Remember, being by Qu is not about diminishing yourself or accepting mistreatment. It's about finding strength, wisdom, and effectiveness through humility, flexibility, and groundedness. As you explore this concept, pay attention to moments when yielding or taking a lower position actually empowers you or leads to better outcomes. These can be opportunities to deepen your understanding and practice of Qu, aligning more closely with the flowing, yielding nature of the Tao.

Chapter 62: Being in the Dao's Cang (Treasure-house)

Within the Dao's vast treasure store,
Lies wisdom deep from shore to shore,
Not gold or gems in coffers sealed,
But truths in every leaf revealed.
The sage, in Cang's abundant space,
Finds riches in each moment's grace,
For in the Dao's eternal wealth,
We touch the source of life itself.

Explanation:

The concept of being in the Dao's Cang (◈), or treasure-house, is a profound idea in Taoist philosophy. It suggests that the Dao itself is an inexhaustible source of wisdom, vitality, and abundance. This treasure-house is not a physical place, but a metaphorical representation of the boundless resources available to those who align themselves with the Dao.

While the Tao Te Ching doesn't explicitly use the term Cang in this context, the idea is implicit in many of Lao Tzu's teachings. For instance, he writes:

"The Tao is like a well:

used but never used up.

It is like the eternal void:

filled with infinite possibilities."

This passage illustrates the inexhaustible nature of the Dao and the abundance available to those who tap into it.

In Taoist thought, the Dao's treasure-house is not filled with material riches, but with the fundamental essences of life and existence. It contains the primordial qi (vital energy), the principles of yin and yang, and the patterns of nature. By attuning ourselves to the Dao, we gain access to this cosmic storehouse of wisdom and vitality.

Being in the Dao's Cang involves more than just intellectual understanding. It's about experientially realizing our connection to the source of all things. This realization brings a sense of abundance, as we recognize that we are part of, and have access to, the infinite resources of the universe.

This concept is closely related to the Taoist practices of meditation and inner alchemy, which aim to cultivate and refine one's internal energies in harmony with the Dao. Through these practices, one learns to draw upon the treasures of the Dao for health, longevity, and spiritual realization.

The idea of the Dao's treasure-house also implies a shift in perspective from scarcity to abundance. When we recognize our connection to the infinite Dao, we no longer feel limited or lacking. Instead, we see opportunities for growth, learning, and fulfillment in every moment and circumstance.

Modern Application:

1. Creativity: Tapping into the infinite source of inspiration and ideas by aligning with the Dao.

2. Problem Solving: Approaching challenges with the understanding that solutions are abundant and available.

3. Personal Growth: Recognizing the limitless potential for development and transformation within oneself.

4. Stress Management: Finding peace in the knowledge that we are connected to an inexhaustible source of strength and resilience.

5. Resource Management: Shifting from a mindset of scarcity to one of abundance and wise stewardship.

6. Learning: Approaching education with curiosity and openness, seeing every experience as an opportunity to access the Dao's wisdom.

7. Health and Wellness: Drawing upon the Dao's vital energy for physical and mental wellbeing.

8. Environmental Awareness: Recognizing the richness and abundance in nature, fostering a deeper respect for the environment.

Practical steps:

- Practicing meditation or qigong to cultivate awareness of the vital energy within and around you
- Regularly spending time in nature to connect with the abundance and wisdom of the natural world
- Keeping a journal of insights and "aha" moments, recognizing them as treasures from the Dao
- Approaching challenges with the question, "What treasure or lesson might the Dao be offering here?"
- Practicing gratitude daily, acknowledging the abundance already present in your life
- Engaging in creative activities without judgment, allowing ideas to flow freely from the Dao's treasure-house
- Before making decisions, taking time to quiet your mind and listen for guidance from the Dao
- Regularly studying Taoist texts or other wisdom traditions to deepen your understanding of universal principles

Reflection Questions:

1. When have you felt most connected to a sense of boundless resources or wisdom? What characterized this experience?

2. How might your life change if you consistently viewed yourself as having access to the Dao's treasure-house?

3. In what areas of your life do you tend to feel scarcity or limitation? How could the concept of the Dao's Cang shift this perspective?

4. How does the idea of an infinite source of wisdom and vitality challenge or support your current worldview?

5. What practices or experiences help you feel most connected to the abundance of the Dao?

6. How could embracing the concept of the Dao's treasure-house enhance your relationships or work life?

7. What might be preventing you from more fully recognizing and drawing upon the treasures of the Dao in your daily life?

Remember, being in the Dao's Cang is not about accumulating knowledge or resources, but about realizing our inherent connection to the source of all things. As you explore this concept, pay attention to moments when you feel a sense of boundless potential or unexpected insight. These can be glimpses of the Dao's treasure-house, inviting you to a deeper, more abundant way of being in the world.

Chapter 63: Being Without Nan (Difficulties)

In life's great flow, no stone can stay,
    As Nan dissolves and fades away,
    Not struggle fierce or burden's weight,
    But ease in which all things equate.
    The sage, in facing every test,
    Finds in each challenge nature's best,
    For in the path without travail,
    We ride the Tao's eternal sail.

Explanation:

Being Without Nan (⬦), or difficulties, is a profound concept in Taoist philosophy. It doesn't suggest a life devoid of challenges, but rather a state of mind and being where what others perceive as difficulties are no longer seen as obstacles. This principle encourages a shift in perspective that allows us to flow with life's events, rather than struggling against them.

While the Tao Te Ching doesn't explicitly use the term Nan in this context, Lao Tzu often speaks about the ease that comes from aligning with the Tao. For instance, he writes:

"The soft overcomes the hard.

The slow overcomes the fast.

Let your workings remain a mystery.

Just show people the results."

This passage illustrates the Taoist view that what seems difficult can be overcome with a different approach – one of softness, patience, and alignment with natural principles.

In Taoist thought, being without difficulties doesn't mean that challenging situations never arise. Instead, it suggests a way of perceiving and interacting with these situations that doesn't create internal resistance or struggle. It's about recognizing that what we often call "difficulties" are simply events or circumstances that don't align with our expectations or desires.

This concept is closely related to the principle of wu wei, or non-action. By not resisting what is, by not labeling situations as difficulties, we can respond more fluidly and effectively to life's challenges. It's about finding the path of least resistance and working with the natural flow of events rather than against it.

Being without Nan also involves a deep trust in the Tao and in one's own nature. When we are in harmony with the Tao, we understand that everything that occurs is part of the natural unfolding of events. From this perspective, there are no difficulties, only opportunities for growth, learning, and further alignment with the Tao.

This principle also encourages us to let go of our attachments to specific outcomes. Many of our perceived difficulties arise from our insistence that things should be different from what they are. By accepting what is and working with it, rather than against it, we can move through life with greater ease and effectiveness.

Modern Application:

1. Stress Management: Reframing challenging situations as opportunities for growth rather than as problems.

2. Problem Solving: Approaching issues with a flexible, open mind that sees multiple possibilities rather than obstacles.

3. Resilience Building: Developing the ability to bounce back from setbacks by not perceiving them as permanent difficulties.

4. Conflict Resolution: Approaching disagreements with a mindset of finding mutual benefit rather than overcoming opposition.

5. Personal Growth: Embracing life's challenges as natural parts of the developmental process rather than as hindrances.

6. Career Development: Viewing career obstacles as opportunities to develop new skills or explore different paths.

7. Relationship Navigation: Seeing relationship challenges as chances to deepen understanding and connection rather than as problems to be solved.

8. Creativity: Approaching creative blocks as opportunities to explore new directions rather than as insurmountable barriers.

Practical steps:

- Practicing mindfulness to observe your reactions to challenging situations without immediate judgment
- When facing a "difficulty," pause and ask, "How might this situation be beneficial?"
- Regularly reflecting on past challenges and identifying the growth or positive outcomes that resulted
- Engaging in practices like tai chi or qigong that teach the principle of yielding and flowing
- Studying nature to observe how natural systems adapt to and work with changing conditions
- Keeping a "challenge journal" where you reframe difficulties as opportunities or learning experiences
- Practicing acceptance of current circumstances before deciding if action is needed

- Developing the habit of looking for multiple perspectives in any challenging situation

Reflection Questions:

1. Can you recall a time when what seemed like a difficulty turned out to be a blessing in disguise? What did this teach you?

2. How might your life change if you no longer perceived anything as a difficulty?

3. What current challenges in your life might you reframe using this Taoist perspective?

4. How does the idea of being without difficulties challenge or support your current approach to personal growth and achievement?

5. Think of someone who seems to embody this quality of being without Nan. How do they approach life differently from others?

6. In what areas of your life do you tend to create the most internal resistance or struggle? How could you apply this principle to those areas?

7. How might embracing this concept affect your relationships and interactions with others?

Remember, being without Nan is not about denying the existence of challenging situations or avoiding necessary action. It's about transforming our perspective and approach to life's events in a way that aligns us more closely with the natural flow of the Tao. As you explore this concept, pay attention to moments when you're able to move through typically "difficult" situations with unexpected ease or insight. These can be glimpses of what it means to be truly without difficulties, in harmony with the Tao's eternal flow.

Chapter 64: Being by Jin Zai (Being Here Now)

In present's grace, all time unfolds,
    As Jin Zai's wisdom gently holds,
    Not past's regret nor future's dream,
    But now, where life and Tao stream.
    The sage, in each unfolding hour,
    Finds in the moment Tao's full power,
    For in the now, both vast and small,
    We touch eternity's soft call.

Explanation:

Jin Zai (◇◇), which can be translated as "being here now" or "present existence," is a fundamental concept in Taoist philosophy that emphasizes the importance of fully inhabiting the present moment. This principle encourages us to anchor our awareness in the here and now, recognizing it as the only true point of contact with reality and the Tao. While the Tao Te Ching doesn't explicitly use the term Jin Zai, the concept of present-moment awareness is implicit in many of Lao Tzu's teachings. For instance, he writes:

"If you realize that all things change,

there is nothing you will try to hold on to.

If you aren't afraid of dying,

there is nothing you can't achieve."

This passage points to the liberation that comes from fully embracing the present, without clinging to the past or anxiously anticipating the future. In Taoist thought, Jin Zai is not just about temporal presence, but about a complete engagement with the fullness of our current experience. It involves a deep recognition that the present moment is our only point of true contact with life and with the Tao. The past exists only in memory, and the future only in imagination – the now is where life actually happens.

This concept is closely related to the Taoist ideal of wu wei, or non-action. By fully inhabiting the present moment, we can respond spontaneously and appropriately to life's circumstances without the hesitation that comes from dwelling on the past or worrying about the future. Being here now also involves a kind of radical acceptance of what is. Instead of resisting our current circumstances or wishing things were different, we fully embrace and engage with the reality of our present situation. This doesn't mean we never plan or reflect, but that we do so from a grounded presence in the now. Jin Zai also points to the Taoist understanding of time as cyclical rather than linear. From this perspective, each moment contains within it the entirety of existence – past, present, and future are all encompassed in the eternal now.

Modern Application:

1. Stress Reduction: Focusing on the present moment to alleviate anxiety about the future or regrets about the past.

2. Productivity: Enhancing focus and efficiency by giving full attention to the task at hand.

3. Relationship Enhancement: Improving the quality of interactions by being fully present with others.

4. Creativity: Accessing deeper wells of inspiration and intuition by immersing fully in the creative process.

5. Decision Making: Making clearer, more grounded choices by assessing situations from a present-centered perspective.

6. Emotional Regulation: Managing emotions more effectively by observing them in the present without getting caught up in past or future narratives.

7. Physical Health: Improving body awareness and responsiveness through present-moment attention.

8. Spiritual Practice: Deepening meditation and contemplative practices by cultivating sustained present-moment awareness.

Practical steps:

- Practicing mindfulness meditation to develop the skill of present-moment awareness
- Using physical sensations (like the breath) as anchors to bring attention back to the present
- Engaging in activities that naturally induce a state of flow or present-moment absorption
- Regularly pausing throughout the day to check in with your current experience
- Practicing mindful eating, savoring each bite and fully experiencing the act of nourishment
- When in conversation, giving full attention to the other person without planning your response
- Engaging in sensory awareness exercises, fully exploring the sights, sounds, smells, tastes, and textures of your environment
- Before bed, reviewing your day with an emphasis on moments when you were fully present

Reflection Questions:

1. When do you feel most fully present in your life? What characterizes these moments?

2. How might your life change if you were consistently able to be here now?

3. What tends to pull your attention away from the present moment most often?

4. How does the idea of the eternal present challenge or support your current understanding of time and existence?

5. Think of someone who seems to embody Jin Zai. How does their presence affect those around them?

6. In what areas of your life could you benefit most from increased present-moment awareness?

7. What fears or attachments might be preventing you from fully embracing the present moment?

Remember, Jin Zai is not about ignoring the past or future, but about fully engaging with life as it unfolds in each moment. As you explore this concept, pay attention to the richness and depth of experience that becomes available when you're fully present. These moments of complete presence can be gateways to a deeper understanding of the Tao and your place within it.

Chapter 65: Being by Chi (Staying Simple-hearted)

In simplicity's pure embrace,
    We find the Tao's eternal grace,
    Chi's wisdom, clear as mountain streams,
    Reveals the truth behind our dreams.
    The sage, with heart uncluttered, free,
    Sees wonder in simplicity,
    For in the clear and open mind,
    The Tao's vast secrets we can find.

Explanation:

Chi (◇), which can be translated as "red" or "bare," is used in Taoist philosophy to represent a state of simplicity, particularly of the heart and mind. Being by Chi, or staying simple-hearted, is about cultivating a pure, uncluttered, and direct way of perceiving and interacting with the world. It's a return to a child-like state of openness and wonder, free from the complications and artifices that often cloud adult perception.

While the Tao Te Ching doesn't explicitly use the term Chi in this context, Lao Tzu often speaks about the virtue of simplicity. For instance, he writes:

"I have just three things to teach:

simplicity, patience, compassion.

These three are your greatest treasures."

This passage highlights the Taoist valuation of simplicity as a key to wisdom and harmony with the Tao. In Taoist thought, staying simple-hearted doesn't mean being simplistic or naive. Rather, it's about maintaining a clear, uncomplicated perspective that allows for direct perception of reality. It's a state where the mind is not cluttered with unnecessary thoughts, prejudices, or complex rationalizations.

This concept is closely related to the Taoist ideal of "uncarved block" or pu (◇). Just as an uncarved block contains all potential forms within it, a simple heart contains all potential understanding. By remaining simple, we stay open to the infinite possibilities of the Tao.

Being by Chi also involves a kind of emotional simplicity. It's about experiencing emotions directly and honestly, without the layers of justification, repression, or elaboration that often complicate our emotional lives. This doesn't mean being emotionally unsophisticated, but rather being emotionally honest and clear.

The simple-hearted approach allows for a more direct and intuitive connection with the Tao. When our hearts and minds are not cluttered with unnecessary complexities, we can more easily align ourselves with the natural flow of life and respond spontaneously and appropriately to each situation.

Modern Application:

1. Decision Making: Cutting through complexity to focus on core issues and values when making choices.

2. Relationships: Fostering more genuine and straightforward interactions, free from hidden agendas or unnecessary complications.

3. Problem Solving: Approaching challenges with a fresh, uncomplicated perspective that can lead to innovative solutions.

4. Stress Reduction: Simplifying one's lifestyle and thought patterns to reduce mental and emotional clutter.

5. Creativity: Accessing more original and authentic forms of expression by bypassing learned conventions and expectations.

6. Spiritual Practice: Cultivating a direct, experiential approach to spirituality rather than getting caught up in dogma or intellectual abstractions.

7. Personal Growth: Focusing on core values and authentic desires rather than societal expectations or complex self-improvement schemes.

8. Communication: Expressing oneself more clearly and honestly, without unnecessary elaboration or obfuscation.

Practical steps:

- Practicing mindfulness to observe the tendency to overcomplicate thoughts and emotions
- Regularly decluttering your physical space as a reflection and support of inner simplicity
- When faced with a decision, asking "What's the simplest solution that addresses the core issue?"
- Engaging in creative activities without judgment, allowing for spontaneous and direct expression
- Practicing speaking plainly and directly, avoiding unnecessary embellishment or equivocation
- Spending time in nature to reconnect with a simpler, more direct way of being
- Regularly reflecting on your core values and using them as a compass for decision making
- Practicing emotional honesty, allowing yourself to feel and express emotions directly

Reflection Questions:

1. When do you feel most simple-hearted in your life? What characterizes these moments?

2. How might your life change if you consistently approached things with a simple, direct perspective?

3. In what areas of your life do you tend to overcomplicate things? What drives this tendency?

4. How does the idea of staying simple-hearted challenge or support your current approach to personal growth and success?

5. Think of someone who embodies Chi, or simple-heartedness. How does their approach to life differ from the norm?

6. How could cultivating a simpler heart enhance your relationships or work life?

7. What fears or beliefs might be preventing you from embracing greater simplicity in your thoughts and emotions?

Remember, being by Chi is not about dumbing down or avoiding complexity when it's truly necessary. It's about cultivating a clear, direct, and uncomplicated way of engaging with life that allows for a more authentic and harmonious existence. As you explore this concept, pay attention to moments when simplicity brings clarity, ease, or a sense of rightness. These can be glimpses of what it means to live with a truly simple heart, in alignment with the Tao.

Chapter 66: Being by Emulating Hai (the Sea)

In depths profound and surface calm,
>   The sea holds wisdom like a psalm,
>   Hai's lessons, vast as oceans wide,
>   Reveal the Tao's eternal tide.
>   The sage, like waters deep and still,
>   Embraces all with boundless will,
>   For in the sea's expansive way,
>   We learn to live the Tao each day.

Explanation:

Emulating Hai (◇), or the sea, is a profound concept in Taoist philosophy that encourages us to model our way of being after the qualities of the ocean. The sea, in Taoist thought, embodies many of the key principles of the Tao – it is vast, deep, adaptable, and powerful, yet it achieves its effects through yielding and flowing rather than through force.

While the Tao Te Ching doesn't explicitly instruct us to emulate the sea, Lao Tzu often uses water as a metaphor for the ideal way of being. He writes:

"The highest good is like water.

Water gives life to the ten thousand things and does not strive.

It flows in places men reject and so is like the Tao."

This passage highlights the Taoist admiration for the qualities of water, which are most fully embodied by the sea.

In Taoist thought, emulating the sea involves several key aspects:

1. Depth and Calmness: Like the sea, which is often calm on the surface even while containing great depths, we can cultivate inner tranquility and depth of character.

2. Adaptability: The sea adapts to any container or shore, teaching us flexibility and the ability to adjust to circumstances without losing our essential nature.

3. Strength through Softness: The sea is immensely powerful, yet it achieves its effects through yielding and flowing rather than through rigid force.

4. Inclusiveness: The sea accepts all rivers and streams without discrimination, teaching us openness and non-judgment.

5. Constancy and Change: While always in motion, the sea remains essentially itself, embodying the balance between change and consistency.

6. Reflection: Like the sea reflecting the sky, we can cultivate a clear, reflective state of mind that mirrors reality without distortion.

7. Rhythmic Nature: The sea's tides teach us about natural cycles and the importance of aligning with the rhythms of nature.

8. Vastness: The immensity of the sea reminds us of the boundless nature of the Tao and encourages us to expand our perspective.

This concept is closely related to the Taoist principle of wu wei, or non-action. Like the sea, which accomplishes great things without striving, we can learn to act effectively without forcing or struggling against the natural flow of events.

Emulating the sea also involves developing a kind of equanimity in the face of life's ups and downs. Just as the sea remains itself whether calm or stormy, we can cultivate an inner stability that isn't easily disturbed by external circumstances.

Modern Application:

1. Emotional Regulation: Developing the ability to remain calm and centered, like the depths of the sea, even when the surface is turbulent.

2. Leadership: Leading with a combination of depth, adaptability, and strength, influencing through presence rather than force.

3. Problem Solving: Approaching challenges with flexibility and persistence, finding ways around obstacles rather than confronting them head-on.

4. Personal Growth: Cultivating depth of character and broadness of perspective, continually expanding one's capacities.

5. Stress Management: Developing resilience and the ability to absorb and dissipate stress, like the sea absorbing impacts.

6. Relationships: Practicing acceptance and inclusivity, welcoming diverse experiences and people without judgment.

7. Creativity: Tapping into the vast depths of the unconscious, allowing ideas to flow and emerge naturally.

8. Environmental Awareness: Recognizing our interconnectedness with all things and the importance of maintaining balance in our ecosystems.

Practical steps:

- Practicing meditation to cultivate inner calmness and depth
- Regularly spending time near bodies of water, observing and reflecting on their qualities
- When faced with challenges, asking "How would the sea approach this?"
- Engaging in activities that promote flow states, like swimming or fluid movement practices
- Practicing acceptance of diverse ideas and people, expanding your circle of compassion

- Keeping a journal to explore the depths of your thoughts and feelings
- Studying the ocean's ecosystems to understand principles of interconnectedness and balance
- In conflicts, experimenting with yielding and flowing around obstacles rather than confronting them directly

Reflection Questions:

1. In what ways do you already embody qualities of the sea? Where could you further develop these qualities?

2. How might your approach to challenges change if you emulated the sea's adaptability and strength through yielding?

3. What aspects of the sea's nature do you find most challenging to emulate? Why?

4. How could cultivating a more sea-like presence enhance your relationships or leadership style?

5. In what areas of your life could you benefit from greater depth or a broader perspective?

6. How does the idea of strength through yielding challenge or support your current understanding of power and effectiveness?

7. What practices or changes could you implement to bring more of the sea's qualities into your daily life?

Remember, being by emulating Hai is not about literally trying to become the sea, but about incorporating its wisdom and qualities into our way of being. As you explore this concept, pay attention to how embodying these qualities affects your interactions with the world and your inner state. The sea, in its vastness and depth, offers a profound model for aligning with the Tao and navigating life with grace and power.

Chapter 67: Being by San Bao (Three Treasures)

In life's grand dance, three jewels shine bright,
San Bao's wisdom, our guiding light,
Compassion, frugality, and humble grace,
In these we find the Tao's embrace.
The sage, in treasuring this trinity,
Unlocks the heart of divinity,
For in these gifts, both small and grand,
We hold the Tao within our hand.

Explanation:

San Bao (□□), or the Three Treasures, is a fundamental concept in Taoist philosophy that outlines three essential virtues or qualities to be cultivated. These treasures, as described by Lao Tzu in the Tao Te Ching, are compassion (ci, □), frugality (jian, □), and humility (bu gan wei tian xia xian, □□□□□□, literally "not daring to be ahead of the world"). Lao Tzu introduces these treasures in Chapter 67 of the Tao Te Ching:

"I have three treasures which I hold and keep.

The first is mercy; the second is economy;

The third is daring not to be ahead of others.

From mercy comes courage; from economy comes generosity;

From humility comes leadership."

These three qualities are seen as the essential attributes that align one with the Tao and allow for harmonious living.

1. Compassion (Ci): This is not just sympathy or pity, but a deep empathy and kindness towards all beings. It's the recognition of our interconnectedness and the practice of treating others as we would want to be treated.

2. Frugality (Jian): This doesn't mean miserliness, but rather a wise and moderate use of resources. It's about recognizing what is enough and not wasting or indulging excessively.

3. Humility (Bu gan wei tian xia xian): This is often translated as "not daring to be ahead of others," which embodies the Taoist value of non-competition and non-assertion. It's about being content with one's place and not striving for superiority or domination.

In Taoist thought, these three treasures are interconnected and mutually reinforcing. Compassion leads to generosity, frugality allows for true giving, and humility creates the space for genuine leadership and influence. The San Bao are not just personal virtues, but principles for harmonious living at all levels – personal, social, and cosmic. They represent a way of being that is in alignment with the Tao, allowing for the natural flow of life and the fulfillment of one's true nature.

Modern Application:

1. Personal Relationships: Practicing compassion, moderation, and humility to foster deeper, more harmonious connections.

2. Leadership: Leading through example, with kindness, resource wisdom, and a non-domineering presence.

3. Environmental Stewardship: Applying frugality in resource use and compassion towards all living beings.

4. Conflict Resolution: Using compassion to understand all sides, humility to seek common ground, and frugality in expending emotional energy on disputes.

5. Personal Growth: Cultivating these virtues as a foundation for genuine self-development and spiritual growth.

6. Financial Management: Practicing wise resource use and generous giving, guided by compassion and humility.

7. Community Building: Fostering a sense of interconnectedness, shared resources, and mutual respect in social groups.

8. Stress Management: Using these principles to create a more balanced, less competitive approach to life.

Practical steps:

- Practicing daily acts of kindness to cultivate compassion
- Regularly assessing your resource use and identifying areas for more frugal living
- When tempted to assert superiority, practicing stepping back and listening instead
- Engaging in volunteer work or community service to embody compassion in action
- Implementing a budget that allows for both wise saving and generous giving
- Practicing active listening in conversations, focusing on understanding rather than being understood
- Regularly reflecting on your motivations: are they driven by compassion, wisdom, and humility?
- Studying nature to observe how these principles operate in natural systems

Reflection Questions:

1. How do you currently embody each of the Three Treasures in your life? Where could you further develop these qualities?

2. How might your approach to challenges change if you consistently applied compassion, frugality, and humility?

3. Which of the Three Treasures do you find most challenging to cultivate? Why?

4. How could embracing these principles enhance your relationships or work life?

5. In what ways might practicing the Three Treasures shift your definition of success or fulfillment?

6. How do these treasures challenge or support your current worldview and values?

7. What practices or changes could you implement to more fully integrate the San Bao into your daily life?

Remember, the Three Treasures are not rigid rules, but guiding principles for aligning with the Tao. As you explore this concept, pay attention to how embodying these qualities affects your inner state and your interactions with the world. The San Bao offer a profound framework for living in harmony with ourselves, others, and the cosmos, embodying the wisdom of the Tao in our everyday lives.

Chapter 68: Being by Tong (Cooperating)

In harmony's sweet, flowing dance,
    Tong's wisdom gives us nature's stance,
    Not conflict's clash or solo's strain,
    But unity in joy and pain.
    The sage, in cooperating flow,
    Lets universal currents grow,
    For in the art of joined hearts' might,
    We touch the Tao day and night.

Explanation:

Tong (◈), which can be translated as "sameness," "togetherness," or "cooperation," is a fundamental concept in Taoist philosophy that emphasizes the importance of harmony, unity, and collaborative effort. This principle recognizes that all things in the universe are interconnected and that true power and effectiveness come from aligning and cooperating with the natural flow of the Tao, rather than struggling against it or attempting to stand alone.

While the Tao Te Ching doesn't explicitly use the term Tong in this context, the concept of cooperation and harmony is central to many of Lao Tzu's teachings. For instance, he writes:

"The Tao of heaven is to take from those who have too much and give to those who do not have enough.

Man's way is different. He takes from those who do not have enough to give to those who already have too much."

This passage illustrates the natural balance and cooperation that exists in the Tao, contrasting it with human tendencies towards competition and accumulation. In Taoist thought, Tong is not about uniformity or the loss of individual identity. Rather, it's about recognizing our fundamental connectedness and learning to work in harmony with others and with the natural world. It's the understanding that we are not isolated entities, but part of a greater whole.

This concept of cooperation extends beyond human relationships to our relationship with nature and the cosmos. It suggests that by aligning ourselves with the natural rhythms and patterns of the universe, we can achieve our goals more effortlessly and harmoniously. Tong also implies a kind of empathy and understanding. When we recognize our sameness or interconnectedness with others, it becomes easier to cooperate, to see from different perspectives, and to find mutually beneficial solutions.

The principle of Tong is closely related to the Taoist concept of wu wei, or non-action. By cooperating with the natural flow of things rather than forcing our will, we can accomplish more with less effort. It's about finding the path of least resistance and moving along it in harmony with others and with nature.

Modern Application:

1. Teamwork: Fostering a collaborative work environment where individuals align their efforts towards common goals.

2. Conflict Resolution: Approaching disagreements with a focus on finding common ground and mutually beneficial solutions.

3. Environmental Stewardship: Recognizing our interconnectedness with nature and working in harmony with natural systems.

4. Community Building: Creating social structures that emphasize cooperation and mutual support rather than competition.

5. Personal Relationships: Cultivating empathy and understanding in our interactions, recognizing our shared humanity.

6. Problem Solving: Approaching challenges with a holistic perspective, considering how all parts of a system can work together.

7. Leadership: Leading through facilitation and alignment rather than through domination or control.

8. Personal Growth: Developing a sense of connection to others and to the larger world as a path to self-realization.

Practical steps:

- Practicing active listening in conversations to better understand and cooperate with others
- Engaging in team-building activities that emphasize collaboration over competition
- When faced with conflicts, looking for win-win solutions rather than trying to "beat" the other side
- Studying ecosystems to understand principles of natural cooperation and applying these in daily life
- Regularly reflecting on your interconnectedness with others and with nature
- Participating in community service or cooperative projects
- In decision-making, considering the impact on all stakeholders and the broader environment
- Practicing mindfulness to develop greater awareness of your place within the larger whole

Reflection Questions:

1. In what areas of your life do you already practice Tong or cooperation? Where could you enhance this practice?

2. How might your approach to challenges change if you consistently sought cooperative solutions?

3. What barriers do you face in fully embracing cooperation in your personal or professional life?

4. How does the idea of cooperating with the natural flow of the Tao challenge or support your current worldview?

5. Think of a time when cooperation led to an unexpectedly positive outcome. What lessons can you draw from this experience?

6. In what ways could embracing Tong enhance your relationships or work life?

7. How might your definition of success or achievement shift if viewed through the lens of cooperation rather than individual accomplishment?

Remember, being by Tong is not about losing your individuality or always agreeing with others. It's about recognizing our fundamental interconnectedness and learning to work in harmony with the natural flow of life and the universe. As you explore this concept, pay attention to moments when cooperation brings ease, effectiveness, or a sense of alignment. These can be glimpses of what it means to truly embody Tong, moving in harmony with the Tao and with all things.

Chapter 69: Being Without Di (Enemies)

In boundless love's embracing light,
    We find no foe, no need to fight,
    Without Di, peace becomes our home,
    As one with all, no more we roam.
    The sage, in seeing friend in all,
    Breaks down division's stubborn wall,
    For in the heart that knows no foe,
    The Tao's eternal love can grow.

Explanation:

Being Without Di (◈), or enemies, is a profound concept in Taoist philosophy that goes beyond the mere absence of conflict. It represents a state of consciousness where one no longer perceives others as adversaries or threats, but rather sees the underlying unity and interconnectedness of all beings. This principle encourages a radical shift in perspective, moving from a mindset of division and opposition to one of harmony and oneness.

While the Tao Te Ching doesn't explicitly use the term Di in this context, Lao Tzu often speaks about the virtues of non-contention and universal love. For instance, he writes:

"The best soldier is not soldierly;

The best fighter is not ferocious;

The best conqueror does not take part in war;

The best employer of men keeps himself below them.

This is called the virtue of not contending;

This is called the power of using men;

This is called matching Heaven, the highest principle of old."

This passage illustrates the Taoist ideal of achieving victory without conflict, of leading without domination, and of living without creating enemies.

In Taoist thought, being without enemies doesn't mean being passive or allowing oneself to be taken advantage of. Rather, it's about transcending the mentality of opposition and recognizing the fundamental sameness in all beings. It's the understanding that what we often perceive as external enemies are often projections of our own inner conflicts or fears.

This concept is closely related to the Taoist principle of wu wei, or non-action. By not creating enemies in our minds, we can respond to challenging situations or people with greater wisdom and effectiveness, without the clouding influence of animosity or fear.

Being without enemies also involves a deep practice of empathy and compassion. When we can see the world from others' perspectives and understand their motivations and struggles, it becomes much harder to view them as enemies, even if we disagree with their actions.

This principle extends beyond human relationships to our relationship with nature and the universe itself. When we see ourselves as part of the great web of life rather than separate from or in opposition to it, we naturally live in greater harmony with all things.

Modern Application:

1. Conflict Resolution: Approaching disagreements with a mindset of mutual understanding rather than opposition.

2. Personal Relationships: Cultivating empathy and compassion in all interactions, even with those we find challenging.

3. Leadership: Leading through inspiration and alignment rather than through force or domination.

4. Social Activism: Working for change through inclusivity and understanding rather than through antagonism.

5. Mental Health: Reducing stress and anxiety by letting go of adversarial thinking patterns.

6. Diplomacy: Fostering international relations based on mutual benefit and understanding rather than competition.

7. Environmental Stewardship: Seeing nature as an ally rather than a resource to be conquered or exploited.

8. Personal Growth: Developing self-acceptance and inner peace by resolving internal conflicts and embracing all aspects of oneself.

Practical steps:

- Practicing loving-kindness meditation to cultivate universal compassion
- When in conflict, pausing to consider the other person's perspective and motivations
- Regularly reflecting on your own projections and how they might be creating perceived enemies
- Engaging in dialogue with those you disagree with, focusing on understanding rather than convincing
- Studying the lives of peace leaders who exemplified the principle of being without enemies
- In daily life, looking for opportunities to transform adversarial relationships into cooperative ones

- Practicing forgiveness, both for others and for yourself
- Cultivating a sense of connection with all beings through mindfulness and contemplation

Reflection Questions:

1. Who do you currently perceive as enemies in your life? How might this perception be limiting you?

2. Can you recall a time when you transformed an enemy into a friend? What allowed this transformation?

3. How might your life change if you truly embraced the concept of being without enemies?

4. What fears or beliefs might be preventing you from seeing the underlying unity in all beings?

5. How could applying this principle enhance your effectiveness in your work or personal life?

6. In what ways does the idea of being without enemies challenge or support your current worldview?

7. What practices or changes could you implement to move towards a state of being without enemies?

Remember, being without Di is not about ignoring real conflicts or differences, but about transcending the mentality of enmity and opposition. As you explore this concept, pay attention to how your perception of others and the world shifts when you let go of the idea of enemies. This practice can lead to a profound sense of peace and alignment with the Tao, transforming not only your external relationships but your inner world as well.

Chapter 70: Being Shen Ming (God-Realized Life)

In sacred union, heaven and earth,
    Shen Ming reveals our divine worth,
    Not distant goal or lofty height,
    But present grace in day and night.
    The sage, in godly essence found,
    Walks holy on most common ground,
    For in the life where Tao's complete,
    Divinity and dust do meet.

Explanation:

Shen Ming (◇◇), which can be translated as "divine clarity" or "spiritual illumination," represents in Taoist philosophy the state of living in full realization of one's divine nature. This concept goes beyond mere intellectual understanding or religious belief; it's about embodying the Tao so completely that one's life becomes a living expression of divine wisdom and harmony.

While the Tao Te Ching doesn't explicitly use the term Shen Ming, the idea of realizing one's oneness with the Tao is central to Taoist thought. Lao Tzu writes:
"Knowing the eternal is called enlightenment.
Not knowing the eternal leads to disaster.
Knowing the eternal renders one all-embracing.
All-embracing means impartial.
Impartial means kingly.
Kingly means heavenly.
Heavenly means one with the Tao.
One with the Tao means eternal.
Though the body dies, there is no danger."
This passage illustrates the Taoist understanding that realizing one's unity with the Tao leads to a state of enlightenment or divine realization.

In Taoist thought, Shen Ming is not about becoming something other than what we are, but about fully realizing our true nature, which is one with the Tao. It's the recognition that divinity is not something external or separate, but the very essence of our being and of all existence.

This state of divine realization is characterized by several qualities:

1. Clarity: A clear perception of reality, unclouded by illusions or delusions.

2. Wisdom: Deep intuitive understanding of the nature of existence.

3. Compassion: Universal love and empathy arising from the recognition of the interconnectedness of all beings.

4. Spontaneity: Effortless, appropriate action in harmony with the Tao.

5. Tranquility: Inner peace and equanimity amidst the fluctuations of life.

6. Unity: A lived experience of oneness with all of existence.

Shen Ming is closely related to the Taoist concept of wu wei, or non-action. In this state of divine realization, one's actions arise spontaneously from one's alignment with the Tao, without the interference of the ego or conceptual mind.

This principle also involves a radical shift in perception, where the sacred and the mundane are no longer seen as separate. In the state of Shen Ming, every aspect of life, no matter how ordinary, is recognized as a manifestation of the divine Tao.

Modern Application:

1. Spiritual Practice: Cultivating a direct, experiential approach to spirituality that goes beyond belief or ritual.

2. Mindfulness: Developing present-moment awareness that recognizes the sacred in everyday experiences.

3. Ethical Living: Basing one's moral choices on a deep, intuitive understanding of interconnectedness and harmony.

4. Creativity: Allowing creative expression to flow from a place of alignment with universal principles.

5. Leadership: Leading from a place of wisdom, compassion, and unity consciousness.

6. Environmental Stewardship: Treating nature with reverence and care, recognizing it as a manifestation of the divine.

7. Personal Relationships: Interacting with others from a place of unconditional love and recognition of shared divine essence.

8. Self-Realization: Pursuing personal growth not as a journey to become something, but as an unfolding of what we already are.

Practical steps:

- Practicing meditation or contemplation to cultivate direct experience of one's divine nature
- Engaging in mindfulness practices to bring awareness to the sacredness of everyday life
- Studying spiritual texts and teachings that point to the divinity within all things
- Regularly reflecting on the interconnectedness of all beings and phenomena
- Practicing seeing the divine in others, especially those we find challenging
- Engaging in creative activities as a form of spiritual expression

- Spending time in nature, cultivating a sense of reverence and connection
- Practicing gratitude for the divine gift of existence in all its forms

Reflection Questions:

1. Have you ever had moments of feeling deeply connected to something greater than yourself? How did these experiences affect you?

2. How might your life change if you consistently recognized and lived from your divine nature?

3. What obstacles do you face in fully embracing the concept of Shen Ming in your daily life?

4. How does the idea of divine realization challenge or support your current spiritual or philosophical views?

5. In what areas of your life do you find it easiest to recognize the sacred? Where do you find it most challenging?

6. How might embracing Shen Ming change your approach to personal growth or achievement?

7. What practices or changes could you implement to cultivate a more God-realized life?

Remember, Shen Ming is not about achieving a special state or becoming superhuman. It's about fully realizing and embodying our true nature, which is one with the Tao. As you explore this concept, pay attention to moments when you feel a sense of deep connection, clarity, or effortless rightness. These can be glimpses of Shen Ming, inviting you into a more profound and divine way of being in the world.

Chapter 71: Being Without Bing (Sickness)

In harmony with Tao's great flow,
    We find the health that sages know,
    Without Bing, life becomes whole,
    As body, mind, and spirit roll.
    The sage, in balance true and deep,
    Knows wellness is for all to keep,
    For in the way of nature's art,
    We heal in every cell and heart.

Explanation:

Being Without Bing (◇), or sickness, is a profound concept in Taoist philosophy that goes beyond mere physical health. It represents a state of holistic wellbeing where one is in perfect harmony with the Tao, resulting in the absence of dis-ease on all levels - physical, mental, emotional, and spiritual.

While the Tao Te Ching doesn't explicitly use the term Bing in this context, Lao Tzu often speaks about the importance of living in accordance with nature and maintaining balance. For instance, he writes:

"The heavy is the root of the light;
The still is the master of unrest.
Therefore the sage, traveling all day,
Does not lose sight of his baggage.
Though there are beautiful things to be seen,
He remains unattached and calm."

This passage illustrates the Taoist ideal of maintaining inner balance and harmony, which is key to being without sickness. In Taoist thought, being without Bing is not just about the absence of physical symptoms, but about a state of profound alignment with the natural order of the universe. This alignment results in a flow of vital energy (qi) that supports health and vitality on all levels.

Key aspects of this concept include:

1. Balance: Maintaining equilibrium between yin and yang forces in the body and life.

2. Prevention: Focusing on maintaining health rather than just treating illness.

3. Holistic Approach: Recognizing the interconnectedness of body, mind, and spirit in health.

4. Natural Healing: Working with the body's innate healing abilities and the healing powers of

nature.

5. Mindful Living: Being aware of how our thoughts, emotions, and actions affect our health.

6. Spiritual Health: Recognizing that true health includes spiritual wellbeing and alignment with the Tao.

7. Environmental Harmony: Understanding that our health is intimately connected with the health of our environment.

This concept is closely related to the Taoist principle of wu wei, or non-action. By living in harmony with the Tao and not resisting the natural flow of life, we can maintain a state of health and balance without forced effort.

Being without Bing also involves a shift in perspective about what health means. Rather than seeing health as a constant battle against disease, it's viewed as our natural state when we're in alignment with the Tao. Illness, from this perspective, is seen as a sign of imbalance or disharmony that needs to be addressed holistically. In Taoist medicine, this principle is applied through practices like qigong, acupuncture, and herbal medicine, which aim to restore balance and promote the free flow of qi throughout the body and being.

Modern Application:

1. Preventive Healthcare: Focusing on lifestyle choices that maintain health rather than just treating symptoms.

2. Stress Management: Recognizing the impact of stress on overall health and practicing techniques to maintain inner balance.

3. Holistic Wellness: Approaching health from a perspective that includes physical, mental, emotional, and spiritual wellbeing.

4. Mindfulness Practices: Cultivating awareness of the body-mind connection and its impact on health.

5. Environmental Health: Recognizing the connection between personal health and the health of our environment.

6. Integrative Medicine: Combining traditional healing wisdom with modern medical knowledge for a more comprehensive approach to health.

7. Workplace Wellness: Creating work environments that support holistic health and prevent stress-related illnesses.

8. Education: Teaching holistic health principles to promote lifelong wellbeing.

Practical steps:

- Practicing qigong, tai chi, or yoga to promote the flow of vital energy
- Adopting a balanced, whole foods diet based on traditional wisdom and modern nutritional science

- Engaging in regular meditation or mindfulness practices to cultivate mental and emotional balance
- Spending time in nature to align with natural rhythms and benefit from the healing power of the natural world
- Regularly assessing and adjusting lifestyle factors to maintain balance (sleep, work, relationships, etc.)
- Learning about and applying principles of Traditional Chinese Medicine in daily life
- Practicing gratitude and positive thinking to support emotional and mental health
- Creating a living and working environment that supports health and vitality

Reflection Questions:

1. How do you currently define health in your life? How might this definition expand by considering the concept of being without Bing?

2. Can you recall a time when you felt in perfect health - not just physically, but mentally, emotionally, and spiritually? What characterized this state?

3. What areas of imbalance or disharmony can you identify in your life that might be impacting your overall health?

4. How might your approach to maintaining health change if you viewed it as your natural state of being in harmony with the Tao?

5. In what ways do your current lifestyle and environment support or hinder your ability to be without Bing?

6. How does the idea of health as a holistic state of being challenge or support your current health practices?

7. What practices or changes could you implement to move towards a state of being without Bing in your life?

Remember, being without Bing is not about achieving a perfect, disease-free state through force of will. It's about aligning ourselves with the natural flow of the Tao, cultivating balance and harmony in all aspects of our being. As you explore this concept, pay attention to moments when you feel a sense of vibrant wellbeing and effortless health. These can be glimpses of what it means to truly be without Bing, in perfect harmony with the Tao.

Chapter 72: Being with Jing (Awe and Acceptance)

In reverence deep and wonder wide,
    With Jing we touch life's sacred side,
    Not blind belief or rigid creed,
    But awe that meets our deepest need.
    The sage, in holy presence still,
    Accepts all with a joyous will,
    For in the dance of yes and wow,
    We greet the Tao in every now.

Explanation:

Being with Jing (◇), which can be translated as "reverence," "respect," or "awe," is a fundamental concept in Taoist philosophy that combines a deep sense of wonder at the mysteries of existence with an attitude of profound acceptance. This principle encourages us to approach life with a sense of sacred appreciation, recognizing the miraculous nature of existence while also accepting its inherent challenges and imperfections.

While the Tao Te Ching doesn't explicitly use the term Jing in this context, Lao Tzu often speaks about the importance of humility and acceptance in the face of the Tao's mysteries. For instance, he writes:

"The Tao that can be told is not the eternal Tao.

The name that can be named is not the eternal name.

The nameless is the beginning of heaven and earth.

The named is the mother of ten thousand things."

This passage illustrates the Taoist recognition of the ultimately mysterious and awe-inspiring nature of existence, which is at the heart of Jing.

In Taoist thought, being with Jing involves several key aspects:

1. Wonder: Cultivating a childlike sense of awe at the beauty and complexity of the universe.

2. Humility: Recognizing our place within the vast cosmic order, neither inflating nor diminishing our significance.

3. Acceptance: Embracing all aspects of life, both pleasant and challenging, as part of the Tao's unfolding.

4. Reverence: Treating all of life, including ourselves, others, and nature, with deep respect.

5. Mystery: Being comfortable with not knowing, and finding joy in the exploration of life's

mysteries.

6. Gratitude: Maintaining an attitude of thankfulness for the gift of existence in all its forms.

This concept is closely related to the Taoist principle of wu wei, or non-action. By cultivating a sense of awe and acceptance, we can align ourselves more easily with the natural flow of the Tao, responding to life with grace and effectiveness.

Being with Jing also involves a kind of radical acceptance that goes beyond mere tolerance or resignation. It's an active embrace of reality as it is, recognizing that even challenging or painful experiences are part of the grand tapestry of existence.

Modern Application:

1. Mindfulness Practice: Cultivating present-moment awareness that allows for a deeper appreciation of everyday experiences.

2. Environmental Stewardship: Approaching nature with a sense of reverence, leading to more sustainable and respectful environmental practices.

3. Conflict Resolution: Bringing an attitude of respect and acceptance to disagreements, facilitating more harmonious resolutions.

4. Personal Growth: Embracing life's challenges as opportunities for learning and development, rather than obstacles to be overcome.

5. Creativity: Tapping into a sense of wonder as a source of inspiration and innovation.

6. Stress Management: Using acceptance as a tool for reducing anxiety about things beyond our control.

7. Relationships: Approaching others with reverence and acceptance, fostering deeper and more authentic connections.

8. Spiritual Practice: Cultivating a sense of the sacred in everyday life, regardless of specific religious beliefs.

Practical steps:

- Practicing mindfulness meditation to develop greater awareness and appreciation of present moments
- Regularly spending time in nature, observing its wonders with childlike curiosity
- Keeping a gratitude journal to cultivate an attitude of thankfulness
- When faced with challenges, practicing acceptance before taking action
- Engaging in contemplative practices that cultivate a sense of awe and mystery
- Regularly expressing appreciation and respect for others
- Studying science or philosophy to deepen your sense of wonder at the complexities of existence
- Practicing art or music as a way of expressing and cultivating reverence for life

Reflection Questions:

1. When do you feel the deepest sense of awe or wonder in your life? How could you cultivate more of these experiences?

2. How might your life change if you approached each moment with a sense of reverence and acceptance?

3. What aspects of life do you find most challenging to accept? How might cultivating Jing change your relationship with these challenges?

4. How does the idea of finding awe in everyday experiences challenge or support your current worldview?

5. In what ways could bringing more reverence into your life enhance your relationships or work?

6. How might practicing Jing change your approach to personal growth or spiritual development?

7. What practices or changes could you implement to cultivate a greater sense of Jing in your daily life?

Remember, being with Jing is not about adopting a particular belief system or forcing a sense of awe. It's about opening ourselves to the inherent wonder and mystery of existence while fully accepting life as it unfolds. As you explore this concept, pay attention to moments when you feel a spontaneous sense of awe or a deep acceptance of what is. These can be glimpses of what it means to truly be with Jing, in harmony with the profound mystery and beauty of the Tao.

Chapter 73: Being in Tian Wang (Heaven's Net)

In cosmic weave, both vast and fine,
Tian Wang holds all by grand design,
Not trap or snare, but loving grace,
That gives each being form and place.
The sage, within this sacred net,
Finds freedom where all needs are met,
For in the mesh of heaven's care,
We dance the Tao beyond compare.

Explanation:

Tian Wang (◇◇), often translated as "Heaven's Net" or "The Net of Heaven," is a profound concept in Taoist philosophy that represents the all-encompassing, interconnected nature of the universe. This metaphorical net is not a constraining force, but rather a supportive structure that holds all of existence in a harmonious, interconnected web.

While the Tao Te Ching doesn't explicitly use the term Tian Wang, Lao Tzu alludes to this concept in various passages. For instance, he writes:

"The net of heaven is vast,
Its meshes are wide, but nothing slips through."

This passage illustrates the Taoist understanding that everything in the universe is caught up in an all-encompassing system of natural law and cosmic order.

In Taoist thought, Tian Wang embodies several key ideas:

1. Interconnectedness: Everything in the universe is intimately connected and influences everything else.

2. Cosmic Justice: There is a natural balance and order to the universe that ultimately accounts for all actions and their consequences.

3. Non-Escapism: No one and nothing can escape the natural laws and processes of the universe.

4. Support: The net is not a trap, but a supportive structure that gives form and place to all beings.

5. Harmony: All parts of the universe work together in a grand, harmonious design.

6. Mystery: The full workings of this cosmic net are beyond human comprehension, invoking a sense of awe and humility.

This concept is closely related to the Taoist principle of wu wei, or non-action. By recognizing our place within Heaven's Net, we can align ourselves more easily with the natural flow of the Tao, acting in harmony with the cosmic order rather than struggling against it.

Being in Tian Wang also involves a profound shift in perspective. It encourages us to see beyond our individual concerns and recognize our place within the larger tapestry of existence. This broader view can bring a sense of peace and acceptance, even in the face of life's challenges.

Modern Application:

1. Ecological Awareness: Recognizing the interconnectedness of all life and the importance of maintaining ecological balance.

2. Ethical Decision-Making: Considering the far-reaching consequences of our actions, recognizing that everything we do affects the whole.

3. Stress Management: Finding peace in the recognition that we are part of a larger order, supported by the universe.

4. Relationship Building: Approaching relationships with an awareness of our interconnectedness and mutual influence.

5. Problem Solving: Taking a holistic approach to challenges, considering the wider context and interconnections.

6. Personal Responsibility: Recognizing that our actions have consequences within the cosmic order, encouraging mindful living.

7. Spiritual Practice: Cultivating a sense of connection with the universe and all beings as a form of spiritual growth.

8. Social Justice: Working towards fairness and equality, recognizing that harm to any part of the net affects the whole.

Practical steps:

- Practicing systems thinking to understand the interconnections in various aspects of life
- Engaging in meditation or contemplation to cultivate a sense of connection with the universe
- Regularly reflecting on the ripple effects of your actions and decisions
- Studying ecology or environmental science to deepen your understanding of natural interconnections
- Practicing mindfulness to become more aware of your place within the larger web of life
- Engaging in acts of kindness, recognizing how positive actions can ripple through the net
- Cultivating patience and trust in natural processes, recognizing that everything has its place and time in the cosmic order
- Regularly expressing gratitude for your place within the grand tapestry of existence

Reflection Questions:

1. How does the concept of Tian Wang change your perspective on your place in the universe?

2. Can you recall a time when you felt deeply connected to the larger web of existence? What characterized this experience?

3. How might your approach to challenges change if you viewed them within the context of Heaven's Net?

4. In what ways do you currently recognize or honor the interconnectedness of all things in your life?

5. How does the idea of cosmic justice or balance challenge or support your current worldview?

6. How might embracing the concept of Tian Wang influence your relationships or your role in your community?

7. What practices or changes could you implement to live more consciously within Heaven's Net?

Remember, being in Tian Wang is not about passivity or fatalism. It's about recognizing our place within the grand cosmic order and acting in harmony with it. As you explore this concept, pay attention to moments when you feel a sense of being held within a larger, supportive structure, or when you recognize the intricate connections between seemingly unrelated events. These can be glimpses of what it means to truly be in Tian Wang, dancing within the vast, beautiful net of the Tao.

Chapter 74: Being with Wu Wei (No Fear of Death)

In life's grand dance, death plays its part,
    Wu Wei reveals the fearless heart,
    Not morbid thought or grim despair,
    But freedom found in death's deep stare.
    The sage, embracing life's full span,
    Fears not the end of mortal man,
    For in the cycle's endless roll,
    We touch the Tao's immortal soul.

Explanation:

Being with Wu Wei (◇◇) in the context of death represents a profound state of fearlessness and acceptance in the face of mortality. This concept goes beyond mere courage; it embodies a deep understanding of the natural cycle of life and death, and an alignment with the eternal nature of the Tao that transcends individual existence.

While the Tao Te Ching doesn't explicitly use the term Wu Wei in this context, Lao Tzu often speaks about the natural cycle of life and death, and the importance of accepting this cycle without fear. For instance, he writes:

"He who knows how to live can walk abroad
Without fear of rhinoceros or tiger.
He will not be wounded in battle.
For in him rhinoceroses can find no place to thrust their horn,
Tigers no place to use their claws,
And weapons no place to pierce.
Why is this so? Because he has no place for death to enter."

This passage illustrates the Taoist view that true fearlessness, including fearlessness of death, comes from a deep alignment with the Tao.

In Taoist thought, being with Wu Wei in relation to death involves several key aspects:

1. Acceptance: Recognizing death as a natural and necessary part of the cosmic cycle.

2. Non-Attachment: Letting go of the ego's desire for permanent individual existence.

3. Transcendence: Understanding that our true nature is one with the eternal Tao, beyond birth and death.

4. Present-Moment Living: Fully engaging with life, unencumbered by the fear of its end.

5. Natural Flow: Aligning with the natural rhythms of life and death without resistance.

6. Wholeness: Seeing life and death as complementary aspects of a greater whole.

This concept is closely related to the broader Taoist principle of wu wei, or non-action. By releasing our fear of death, we can live more fully and authentically, acting in harmony with the natural flow of existence.

Being with Wu Wei in the face of death also involves a shift in perspective about the nature of existence. Rather than seeing ourselves as separate entities struggling against mortality, we recognize our place within the eternal dance of the Tao, where forms arise and dissolve in an ongoing cycle of transformation.

Modern Application:

1. End-of-Life Care: Approaching death with dignity, peace, and acceptance, both for oneself and when supporting others.

2. Risk Assessment: Making life choices based on values and meaning rather than fear of mortality.

3. Stress Reduction: Alleviating anxiety related to death and impermanence.

4. Grief Processing: Finding peace and acceptance when dealing with the loss of loved ones.

5. Life Purpose: Living more fully and authentically by releasing the fear of death.

6. Medical Ethics: Informing discussions and decisions about life-prolonging treatments and quality of life.

7. Environmental Awareness: Recognizing our place within the larger cycle of nature, including death and renewal.

8. Spiritual Practice: Deepening spiritual understanding by contemplating and accepting the reality of death.

Practical steps:

- Practicing meditation on impermanence to cultivate acceptance of life's transient nature
- Engaging in death awareness practices, such as the Tibetan maranasati (mindfulness of death)
- Regularly reflecting on your life's meaning and purpose, independent of its duration
- Studying philosophical or spiritual teachings on death and impermanence
- Volunteering in hospice or end-of-life care to become more comfortable with the reality of death
- Creating a "bucket list" and actively working towards meaningful life experiences
- Practicing letting go of attachments in daily life as a way to prepare for the ultimate letting go
- Engaging in conversations about death and dying to reduce taboo and fear

Reflection Questions:

1. How does your current relationship with death affect the way you live your life?

2. Can you recall a time when acceptance of mortality brought you a sense of peace or freedom? What characterized this experience?

3. How might your life change if you truly lived without fear of death?

4. In what ways does the idea of being one with the eternal Tao challenge or support your current views on death and afterlife?

5. How could embracing Wu Wei in relation to death enhance your relationships or your approach to life's challenges?

6. What fears or attachments might be preventing you from fully accepting the reality of death?

7. How might your priorities or life choices shift if you lived with a constant awareness of mortality?

Remember, being with Wu Wei in relation to death is not about becoming morbid or obsessed with mortality. It's about embracing the full cycle of existence, including its end, as a way to live more fully and authentically. As you explore this concept, pay attention to moments when acceptance of impermanence brings a sense of peace, freedom, or heightened appreciation for life. These can be glimpses of what it means to truly be with Wu Wei, dancing with both life and death in the eternal flow of the Tao.

Chapter 75: Being by Shao Qiu (Demanding Little)

In simplicity's embrace we find,
The wealth that truly frees the mind,
Shao Qiu, the art of asking less,
Reveals the path to true success.
The sage, content with what's at hand,
Needs not the riches of the land,
For in the way of least demand,
We touch the Tao's abundant strand.

Explanation:

Shao Qiu (￿￿), which can be translated as "demanding little" or "seeking less," is a fundamental principle in Taoist philosophy that emphasizes the virtue of contentment and the wisdom of minimizing desires. This concept goes beyond mere frugality; it represents a profound shift in our relationship with the world, encouraging us to find fulfillment in simplicity rather than in accumulation or achievement.

While the Tao Te Ching doesn't explicitly use the term Shao Qiu, Lao Tzu often speaks about the virtues of simplicity and non-striving. For instance, he writes:

"He who knows he has enough is rich.
Perseverance is a sign of willpower.
He who stays where he is endures.
To die but not to perish is to be eternally present."

This passage illustrates the Taoist view that true wealth and endurance come from contentment and stability, not from constant seeking or accumulation.

In Taoist thought, being by Shao Qiu involves several key aspects:

1. Contentment: Finding satisfaction and joy in what one already has.

2. Simplicity: Valuing a straightforward, uncluttered way of life.

3. Non-Striving: Releasing the constant drive for more or better.

4. Natural Sufficiency: Trusting in the abundance of the Tao and one's own innate completeness.

5. Clarity: Distinguishing between genuine needs and conditioned wants.

6. Freedom: Liberating oneself from the tyranny of desires and societal expectations.

7. Appreciation: Cultivating gratitude for the simple gifts of existence.

This concept is closely related to the Taoist principle of wu wei, or non-action. By demanding little, we align ourselves more easily with the natural flow of the Tao, finding effortless effectiveness and peace.

Shao Qiu also involves a shift in our understanding of wealth and success. Instead of measuring these in terms of material possessions or achievements, they are gauged by inner peace, harmony with the Tao, and the richness of simple experiences.

This principle doesn't advocate for deprivation or asceticism, but rather for finding the point of "enough" - the place where our genuine needs are met without excess or waste. It's about recognizing that often, in seeking more, we lose appreciation for what we already have.

Modern Application:

1. Minimalism: Embracing a lifestyle that focuses on simplicity and the elimination of excess.

2. Financial Wellbeing: Developing a healthier relationship with money, focusing on sufficiency rather than excess.

3. Stress Reduction: Alleviating anxiety related to constant striving and the pressure to acquire or achieve.

4. Environmental Sustainability: Reducing consumption and waste by being content with less.

5. Time Management: Freeing up time and energy by reducing unnecessary pursuits and possessions.

6. Mental Clarity: Clearing mental clutter by reducing desires and simplifying one's life focus.

7. Relationship Enhancement: Fostering deeper connections by valuing presence and simplicity over materialism.

8. Work-Life Balance: Redefining success to include contentment and life quality, not just career advancement.

Practical steps:

- Regularly practicing gratitude for what you already have
- Conducting a "life audit" to identify and eliminate unnecessary possessions or commitments
- Implementing a "one in, one out" rule for new acquisitions to maintain simplicity
- Experimenting with periods of voluntary simplicity or fasting from certain comforts
- Before making purchases, pausing to reflect on whether the item is truly needed
- Cultivating hobbies and interests that don't require significant material resources
- Practicing mindfulness to become more aware of the richness of simple, present-moment experiences
- Regularly reassessing your definition of "enough" in various areas of life

Reflection Questions:

1. What truly brings you contentment in life? How often do you prioritize these things?

2. Can you recall a time when having or wanting less actually led to greater satisfaction? What did this teach you?

3. How might your life change if you consistently practiced Shao Qiu?

4. What fears or beliefs might be driving a need for more in certain aspects of your life?

5. How does the idea of "success through wanting less" challenge or support your current goals and aspirations?

6. In what areas of your life do you find it most challenging to practice Shao Qiu? Why?

7. How could embracing this principle enhance your relationships or your sense of purpose?

Remember, being by Shao Qiu is not about depriving yourself or rejecting the world. It's about finding freedom, peace, and fulfillment through simplicity and contentment. As you explore this concept, pay attention to moments when desiring or acquiring less brings a sense of lightness, clarity, or joy. These can be glimpses of what it means to truly embody Shao Qiu, finding abundance in simplicity and alignment with the Tao.

Chapter 76: Being by Qu (Bending)

In flexibility's gentle art,

   We find the strength that sets us apart,

   Qu's wisdom, like the willow tree,

   Teaches how to bend and be free.

   The sage, in yielding, finds true might,

   Flows with the Tao both day and night,

   For in the way of supple grace,

   We dance with life in every place.

Explanation:

Qu (◇), which can be translated as "to bend" or "to yield," is a fundamental concept in Taoist philosophy that emphasizes the power of flexibility and adaptability. This principle teaches that true strength often lies not in rigid resistance, but in the ability to bend without breaking, to adapt to circumstances while maintaining one's essential nature.

While the Tao Te Ching doesn't explicitly use the term Qu in this context, Lao Tzu often speaks about the strength of softness and the wisdom of yielding. For instance, he writes:

"The soft overcomes the hard;

the gentle overcomes the rigid.

Everyone knows this is true,

but few can put it into practice."

This passage illustrates the Taoist understanding that flexibility and gentleness, paradoxically, can be more powerful and enduring than hardness and force.

In Taoist thought, being by Qu involves several key aspects:

1. Adaptability: The ability to adjust to changing circumstances without losing one's core essence.

2. Resilience: Bouncing back from adversity by bending rather than breaking.

3. Non-Resistance: Flowing with rather than against the natural currents of life.

4. Strategic Yielding: Knowing when to give way in order to ultimately prevail.

5. Softness as Strength: Recognizing that gentleness and flexibility can be more powerful than rigidity and force.

6. Natural Alignment: Emulating the flexibility seen in nature, such as trees that bend in the wind.

7. Preservation of Energy: Conserving strength by not resisting unnecessarily.

This concept is closely related to the Taoist principle of wu wei, or non-action. By being flexible and yielding, we can achieve our aims more effortlessly and in greater harmony with the Tao.

Qu also involves a shift in how we view strength and power. Instead of seeing power as the ability to impose one's will or resist change, it's understood as the capacity to adapt, to flow with circumstances, and to maintain one's integrity even while being flexible.

This principle doesn't mean being weak or passive. Rather, it's about cultivating a kind of strength that is responsive, adaptable, and ultimately more resilient. Like water that can wear away stone or a young sapling that bends in the wind while the rigid old tree breaks, the power of Qu lies in its ability to persist and prevail through flexibility.

Modern Application:

1. Stress Management: Developing resilience by learning to 'bend' rather than break under pressure.

2. Conflict Resolution: Approaching disagreements with a willingness to yield on non-essentials while maintaining core principles.

3. Career Development: Adapting to changing job markets and work environments while staying true to personal values.

4. Personal Relationships: Cultivating flexibility in interactions, allowing for compromise and mutual growth.

5. Problem Solving: Approaching challenges with a flexible mindset, willing to adapt strategies as needed.

6. Leadership: Leading with adaptability, able to adjust approaches based on team needs and changing circumstances.

7. Physical Health: Understanding the importance of flexibility alongside strength in physical fitness.

8. Mental Health: Developing psychological flexibility to better cope with life's uncertainties and changes.

Practical steps:

- Practicing yoga or tai chi to experience physical flexibility as a metaphor for mental and emotional flexibility
- When faced with opposition, experimenting with yielding or redirecting energy rather than meeting force with force
- Regularly putting yourself in new situations that require adaptability
- In conflicts, practicing looking for areas where you can be flexible without compromising core values
- Studying nature to observe how plants and animals demonstrate flexibility and adaptation

- Engaging in improvisational activities (like music or theater) to cultivate spontaneity and adaptability
- Practicing mindfulness to become more aware of when you're being rigid and could benefit from more flexibility
- Regularly reflecting on situations where being flexible led to positive outcomes

Reflection Questions:

1. Can you recall a time when being flexible or yielding led to a better outcome than being rigid or forceful? What did this teach you?

2. In what areas of your life do you tend to be most rigid? How might cultivating more flexibility in these areas benefit you?

3. How does the idea of strength through flexibility challenge or support your current understanding of power and effectiveness?

4. Think of someone you know who embodies the quality of Qu. How does their flexibility manifest in their life and relationships?

5. How might embracing Qu change your approach to current challenges or goals in your life?

6. What fears or beliefs might be preventing you from being more flexible in certain situations?

7. How could practicing Qu enhance your relationships or work life?

Remember, being by Qu is not about being spineless or always giving in. It's about cultivating a kind of strength that is adaptable, resilient, and in harmony with the natural flow of the Tao. As you explore this concept, pay attention to moments when yielding or being flexible feels more powerful than resisting or forcing. These can be opportunities to deepen your understanding and practice of Qu in your daily life, leading to a more harmonious and effective way of navigating the world.

Chapter 77: Being by Yu Yu (Offering the Surplus)

In giving's grace, we find our way,
    Yu Yu teaches us to not delay,
    To share our bounty, large or small,
    And answer to the cosmos' call.
    The sage, in offering what's spare,
    Finds richness beyond compare,
    For in the flow of give and take,
    We let the Tao through us awake.

Explanation:

Yu Yu (◇◇), which can be translated as "offering the surplus" or "giving from abundance," is a profound concept in Taoist philosophy that emphasizes the virtue of generosity and the wisdom of circulating resources. This principle goes beyond mere charity; it represents a fundamental understanding of the flow of energy and resources in the universe and our role in facilitating this flow.

While the Tao Te Ching doesn't explicitly use the term Yu Yu, Lao Tzu often speaks about the virtues of giving and non-attachment. For instance, he writes:

"The sage does not accumulate for himself.

The more he uses for others, the more he has himself.

The more he gives to others, the more he possesses of his own."

This passage illustrates the Taoist view that true abundance comes not from hoarding, but from participating in the natural flow of giving and receiving.

In Taoist thought, being by Yu Yu involves several key aspects:

1. Recognizing Abundance: Understanding that we often have more than we need.

2. Non-Attachment: Letting go of the urge to accumulate or hoard resources.

3. Facilitating Flow: Participating in the natural circulation of energy and resources in the universe.

4. Trust: Having faith that by giving, we participate in a larger system of exchange that will also support us.

5. Harmony: Aligning ourselves with the natural principles of balance and circulation in the cosmos.

6. Generosity: Cultivating a spirit of giving and sharing as a way of life.

7. Awareness: Being attentive to opportunities to offer our surplus to others.

This concept is closely related to the Taoist principle of wu wei, or non-action. By freely offering our surplus, we align ourselves with the natural flow of the Tao, allowing resources to circulate effortlessly and beneficially.

Yu Yu also involves a shift in our understanding of wealth and abundance. Instead of measuring wealth by what we accumulate, it's gauged by our capacity to give and our participation in the flow of resources. This principle recognizes that true abundance is not static, but dynamic – it's found in the movement and sharing of resources rather than in their accumulation.

It's important to note that Yu Yu is not about giving everything away or neglecting one's own needs. It's about recognizing when we have more than we need and being willing to share that surplus. This could be material resources, but it could also be time, knowledge, skills, or even positive energy.

Modern Application:

1. Resource Management: Developing a more fluid and generous approach to managing personal and organizational resources.

2. Environmental Stewardship: Recognizing our responsibility to share and circulate resources in a way that benefits the larger ecosystem.

3. Community Building: Fostering stronger communities through a culture of sharing and mutual support.

4. Personal Growth: Cultivating generosity as a path to greater fulfillment and connection with others.

5. Business Ethics: Developing business models that prioritize giving back and creating value for all stakeholders.

6. Stress Reduction: Alleviating anxiety related to scarcity by recognizing and sharing from our abundance.

7. Creativity: Sharing ideas and inspirations freely, recognizing that creativity flourishes in an open, generous environment.

8. Spiritual Practice: Deepening spiritual understanding through the practice of generosity and non-attachment.

Practical steps:

- Regularly assessing your resources (material, time, skills, etc.) to identify areas of surplus
- Implementing a practice of regular giving or volunteering
- When making purchases, considering buying extra to share with others in need
- Practicing knowledge sharing in your professional or personal life
- Cultivating a mindset of abundance by regularly acknowledging what you have
- Participating in or initiating community sharing programs or initiatives
- When receiving, thinking of ways to pass on the benefit to others

- Regularly decluttering and donating unused items

Reflection Questions:

1. In what areas of your life do you currently have a surplus? How might you share this with others?

2. Can you recall a time when giving from your abundance led to unexpected positive outcomes? What did this teach you?

3. How might your life change if you consistently practiced Yu Yu?

4. What fears or beliefs might be preventing you from sharing your surplus more freely?

5. How does the idea of "wealth through giving" challenge or support your current views on abundance and success?

6. In what ways could embracing Yu Yu enhance your relationships or sense of purpose?

7. How might practicing Yu Yu change your approach to work, creativity, or problem-solving?

Remember, being by Yu Yu is not about self-deprivation or forced charity. It's about recognizing our inherent abundance and joyfully participating in the natural flow of giving and receiving. As you explore this concept, pay attention to moments when sharing brings a sense of fulfillment, connection, or increased abundance. These can be glimpses of what it means to truly embody Yu Yu, aligning with the generous, flowing nature of the Tao.

Chapter 78: Being like Shui (Water)

In water's flow, we find our way,

   Shui's wisdom guides us day by day,

   Not force or strife, but gentle might,

   That shapes the world both day and night.

   The sage, in liquid grace divine,

   Lets go of self to intertwine,

   For in the stream of formless form,

   We ride the Tao through calm and storm.

Explanation:

Being like Shui (◈), or water, is a central concept in Taoist philosophy that embodies the ideal way of being and interacting with the world. Water, in Taoist thought, exemplifies many of the key virtues and principles of the Tao, serving as a powerful metaphor for how to live in harmony with the natural order of the universe. Lao Tzu explicitly praises the qualities of water in the Tao Te Ching:

"The highest good is like water.

Water gives life to the ten thousand things and does not strive.

It flows in places men reject and so is like the Tao."

This passage highlights the Taoist admiration for water's ability to nourish all things while remaining humble and adaptable.

In Taoist philosophy, being like Shui involves embodying several key qualities:

1. Adaptability: Water takes the shape of any container it's in, teaching us to be flexible and adapt to circumstances without losing our essential nature.

2. Softness and Strength: Water is soft and yielding, yet over time it can wear away even the hardest stone, demonstrating that gentleness can be more powerful than force.

3. Humility: Water always seeks the lowest places, yet it's essential for all life, showing that true power often lies in humility and service.

4. Persistence: Water flows continuously, finding a way around obstacles rather than confronting them directly, teaching persistence and patience.

5. Purification: Water has the ability to cleanse and purify, reminding us of the importance of maintaining inner purity and clarity.

6. Reflectiveness: A calm water surface reflects the world around it perfectly, symbolizing the clear, unbiased mind of the sage.

7. Unity: Water droplets naturally come together to form larger bodies, demonstrating the principle of unity and interconnectedness.

8. Non-Contention: Water does not compete or struggle, yet it accomplishes great things, embodying the principle of wu wei or non-action.

This concept is closely related to the Taoist principle of wu wei, as water exemplifies effortless action. By emulating water, we learn to act in harmony with the natural flow of the Tao, achieving our aims without forced effort or struggle. Being like Shui also involves a shift in how we view strength and effectiveness. Instead of seeing power as the ability to dominate or control, it's understood as the capacity to flow, adapt, and persevere. This principle teaches that true strength often lies in flexibility, humility, and the ability to work with rather than against the natural order of things.

Modern Application:

1. Leadership: Developing a leadership style that is adaptable, nurturing, and works with rather than against team dynamics.

2. Conflict Resolution: Approaching disagreements with a fluid, adaptable mindset, finding ways around obstacles rather than confronting them head-on.

3. Personal Growth: Cultivating flexibility, persistence, and humility in personal development.

4. Stress Management: Learning to "go with the flow" and adapt to changing circumstances rather than resisting them.

5. Problem Solving: Approaching challenges with a flexible, adaptive mindset, willing to find unconventional solutions.

6. Relationships: Cultivating the ability to adapt to others' needs while maintaining one's own integrity, like water taking the shape of its container.

7. Creativity: Allowing ideas to flow freely and adapt to new forms, like water finding its way through any terrain.

8. Environmental Awareness: Understanding and working with natural processes rather than trying to control or dominate them.

Practical steps:

- Practicing mindfulness of water in daily life, observing its qualities and behaviors
- Engaging in water-based activities like swimming or sailing to experience water's qualities directly
- When faced with obstacles, asking "How would water approach this situation?"
- Practicing tai chi or qigong, which often incorporate water-like movements
- In conflicts, experimenting with "flowing around" obstacles rather than confronting them directly
- Cultivating a daily practice of letting go, like water releasing its form to take on a new one

- Regularly reflecting on how you can be more adaptable, humble, or persistent in various life situations
- Studying the water cycle and other natural water phenomena to deepen your understanding of water's wisdom

Reflection Questions:

1. In what areas of your life do you already embody water-like qualities? Where could you benefit from being more like water?

2. Can you recall a situation where adopting a water-like approach led to a positive outcome? What did this teach you?

3. How might your approach to challenges change if you consistently emulated the qualities of water?

4. What aspects of water's nature do you find most challenging to emulate? Why?

5. How could cultivating a more water-like presence enhance your relationships or leadership style?

6. In what ways does the idea of strength through softness and adaptability challenge or support your current understanding of power and effectiveness?

7. What practices or changes could you implement to bring more of water's qualities into your daily life?

Remember, being like Shui is not about losing one's identity or always giving way. It's about cultivating a way of being that is adaptable, persistent, and in harmony with the natural flow of the Tao. As you explore this concept, pay attention to how embodying these qualities affects your interactions with the world and your inner state. Water, in its simplicity and profundity, offers a powerful model for aligning with the Tao and navigating life with grace and effectiveness.

Chapter 79: Being Without Yuan (Resentments)

In forgiveness' light, we find our way,
  As Yuan dissolves like mist at day,
  Not grudge or spite, but freedom's grace,
  That opens heart to Tao's embrace.
  The sage, unburdened by the past,
  Lets go of wrongs from first to last,
  For in release of every slight,
  We touch the Tao's eternal light.

Explanation:

Being Without Yuan (◇), or resentments, is a profound concept in Taoist philosophy that emphasizes the importance of letting go of grudges, grievances, and negative feelings towards others or situations. This principle recognizes that holding onto resentments not only harms our own well-being but also disrupts our harmony with the Tao and with others. While the Tao Te Ching doesn't explicitly use the term Yuan in this context, Lao Tzu often speaks about the virtues of non-contention and harmony. For instance, he writes:

"The best way to settle an argument is to avoid it altogether."

This passage illustrates the Taoist preference for avoiding conflict and the accumulation of resentments in the first place.

In Taoist thought, being without Yuan involves several key aspects:

1. Forgiveness: The ability to let go of past hurts and grievances.

2. Non-Attachment: Not clinging to negative emotions or experiences.

3. Understanding: Recognizing that all actions arise from complex causes and conditions.

4. Acceptance: Embracing life's experiences without judgment or resistance.

5. Harmony: Maintaining inner and outer peace by releasing resentments.

6. Wisdom: Seeing the futility of holding onto grievances.

7. Freedom: Liberating oneself from the burden of past wrongs.

This concept is closely related to the Taoist principle of wu wei, or non-action. By letting go of resentments, we align ourselves more easily with the natural flow of the Tao, responding to life's challenges with greater ease and effectiveness. Being without Yuan also involves a shift in how we view justice and interpersonal dynamics. Instead of seeking retribution or holding onto grievances, it encourages us to find ways to restore harmony and move forward. This doesn't mean ignoring injustice, but rather addressing it in ways that don't perpetuate cycles of negativity and resentment.

It's important to note that being without Yuan is not about suppressing emotions or denying the reality of hurtful experiences. Rather, it's about processing these experiences in a way that allows us to release their negative hold on us and move forward in harmony with the Tao.

Modern Application:

1. Conflict Resolution: Approaching disagreements with a focus on understanding and reconciliation rather than blame.

2. Mental Health: Releasing resentments as a way to reduce stress, anxiety, and depression.

3. Relationships: Cultivating forgiveness and understanding to build stronger, more resilient connections.

4. Personal Growth: Using challenging experiences as opportunities for learning and development rather than sources of ongoing resentment.

5. Leadership: Creating environments that focus on solutions and growth rather than blame and punishment.

6. Social Justice: Working towards change from a place of compassion and understanding rather than anger or resentment.

7. Stress Management: Letting go of resentments as a way to reduce emotional and physical stress.

8. Spiritual Practice: Deepening spiritual understanding through the practice of forgiveness and non-attachment.

Practical steps:

- Practicing mindfulness to become aware of resentments as they arise
- Engaging in forgiveness meditation or exercises
- When feeling resentful, pausing to consider the other person's perspective or circumstances
- Regularly reflecting on past resentments and consciously choosing to release them
- Practicing expressing feelings and needs clearly to avoid the build-up of resentments
- Engaging in physical practices like yoga or tai chi that encourage the release of tension and negative emotions
- Journaling about resentments and exploring ways to transform these feelings
- Seeking therapy or counseling to work through deep-seated resentments or traumas

Reflection Questions:

1. What resentments are you currently holding onto? How are these affecting your life and relationships?

2. Can you recall a time when letting go of a resentment led to a positive outcome? What did this experience teach you?

3. How might your life change if you consistently practiced being without Yuan?

4. What fears or beliefs might be preventing you from letting go of certain resentments?

5. How does the idea of addressing injustice without holding onto resentment challenge or support your current views on justice and conflict resolution?

6. In what ways could embracing this principle enhance your relationships or sense of inner peace?

7. How might practicing being without Yuan change your approach to personal growth or spiritual development?

Remember, being without Yuan is not about ignoring injustice or suppressing legitimate grievances. It's about finding ways to address these issues without being burdened by ongoing resentment. As you explore this concept, pay attention to moments when letting go of a resentment brings a sense of freedom, peace, or renewed energy. These can be glimpses of what it means to truly embody being without Yuan, aligning with the harmonious, flowing nature of the Tao.

Chapter 80: Being Your Own Tien Xia (Utopia)

In inner realms, a kingdom grand,
Tien Xia blooms at your command,
Not distant dream or far-off shore,
But here and now, forevermore.
The sage, in self a world complete,
Finds heaven where the heart does beat,
For in the soul's vast, boundless space,
We build the Tao's most perfect place.

Explanation:

Being Your Own Tien Xia (◇◇), which literally translates to "under heaven" but is often interpreted as "utopia" or "ideal world," is a profound concept in Taoist philosophy that emphasizes the importance of cultivating inner harmony and perfection rather than seeking it in the external world. This principle suggests that the ideal state of being is not found in some distant, perfect society, but within oneself, through alignment with the Tao.

While the Tao Te Ching doesn't explicitly use the term Tien Xia in this context, Lao Tzu often speaks about the virtues of simplicity, contentment, and inner cultivation. For instance, he writes:
"Without going outside his door, one understands all that takes place under the sky;
Without looking out from his window, one sees the way of heaven.
The further one goes, the less one knows."
This passage illustrates the Taoist view that true wisdom and perfection are found within, not in external pursuits.

In Taoist thought, being your own Tien Xia involves several key aspects:

1. Inner Cultivation: Focusing on developing one's inner world rather than trying to perfect the external world.

2. Self-Sufficiency: Finding contentment and fulfillment within oneself rather than depending on external circumstances.

3. Harmony: Aligning one's inner state with the principles of the Tao.

4. Simplicity: Embracing a simple, authentic way of being rather than striving for complex ideals.

5. Presence: Fully inhabiting and appreciating the present moment rather than yearning for a future utopia.

6. Wholeness: Recognizing and integrating all aspects of oneself, including perceived flaws.

7. Microcosm: Understanding that one's inner world reflects and influences the outer world.

This concept is closely related to the Taoist principle of wu wei, or non-action. By cultivating inner perfection, we naturally align ourselves with the Tao, influencing the world around us without forced effort.

Being your own Tien Xia also involves a shift in how we view perfection and ideals. Instead of projecting our visions of perfection onto the external world or future scenarios, we learn to find and cultivate the seeds of perfection within our own being, in the present moment.

It's important to note that this principle doesn't advocate for disengagement from the world or neglect of social responsibilities. Rather, it suggests that the most effective way to create positive change in the world is to first cultivate harmony and alignment within oneself.

Modern Application:

1. Personal Development: Focusing on inner growth and self-improvement rather than comparing oneself to others or external standards.

2. Stress Management: Finding peace and contentment within, regardless of external circumstances.

3. Leadership: Cultivating inner qualities that naturally inspire and positively influence others.

4. Creativity: Tapping into one's inner world as a source of unique expression and innovation.

5. Relationships: Developing self-sufficiency and inner harmony as a foundation for healthy, balanced relationships.

6. Social Change: Understanding that societal transformation begins with personal transformation.

7. Mental Health: Cultivating inner resources for emotional stability and resilience.

8. Spiritual Practice: Deepening spiritual understanding by exploring the vastness of one's inner world.

Practical steps:

- Practicing daily meditation or self-reflection to cultivate inner awareness
- Creating a personal sanctuary or space that reflects your ideal inner state
- Regularly assessing and aligning your actions with your inner values
- Engaging in creative activities that express your inner world
- Practicing gratitude for the present moment and your current circumstances
- Cultivating mindfulness to fully inhabit and appreciate your inner and outer experiences
- Exploring practices like yoga or qigong that connect inner states with physical expression
- Journaling about your vision of an ideal inner world and steps to manifest it

Reflection Questions:

1. What does your personal "utopia" look like? How much of this is dependent on external factors versus internal states?

2. Can you recall a time when you felt completely at peace and content within yourself? What characterized this experience?

3. How might your life change if you consistently viewed yourself as your own Tien Xia?

4. What internal obstacles do you face in cultivating your ideal inner state?

5. How does the idea of creating change through inner cultivation challenge or support your current views on personal and social transformation?

6. In what ways could embracing this principle enhance your relationships or sense of purpose?

7. How might practicing being your own Tien Xia change your approach to challenges or goals in your external life?

Remember, being your own Tien Xia is not about escaping reality or becoming self-centered. It's about recognizing that the seeds of perfection and harmony exist within us, and that by cultivating these internal qualities, we can naturally bring more beauty and balance to the world around us. As you explore this concept, pay attention to moments when you feel a sense of inner completeness or harmony. These can be glimpses of what it means to truly embody your own Tien Xia, aligning with the perfect, complete nature of the Tao within yourself.

Chapter 81: Being Without Ji Ji (Accumulating)

In letting go, we truly gain,
    As Ji Ji's illusion wanes,
    Not hoarding wealth or worldly things,
    But free in what each moment brings.
    The sage, unburdened by excess,
    Finds richness in life's simpleness,
    For in release of all we cling,
    We touch the Tao in everything.

Explanation:

Being Without Ji Ji (◇◇), or accumulating, is a fundamental concept in Taoist philosophy that emphasizes the wisdom of non-attachment and the folly of excessive accumulation. This principle recognizes that the drive to constantly acquire and hoard – whether material possessions, knowledge, or even spiritual merits – can actually hinder our alignment with the Tao and our experience of true fulfillment.

While the Tao Te Ching doesn't explicitly use the term Ji Ji, Lao Tzu often speaks about the virtues of simplicity and non-attachment. For instance, he writes:

"To attain knowledge, add things every day.

To attain wisdom, remove things every day."

This passage illustrates the Taoist view that true wisdom often comes from letting go rather than accumulating.

In Taoist thought, being without Ji Ji involves several key aspects:

1. Non-Attachment: Releasing the urge to possess and hold onto things.

2. Simplicity: Valuing a life uncluttered by excess possessions or concerns.

3. Flow: Allowing resources and energy to circulate freely rather than hoarding them.

4. Contentment: Finding satisfaction in what is, rather than always seeking more.

5. Presence: Fully experiencing the present moment instead of accumulating for the future.

6. Trust: Having faith in the abundance of the Tao rather than stockpiling out of fear.

7. Freedom: Liberating oneself from the burden of excess and the anxiety of acquisition.

This concept is closely related to the Taoist principle of wu wei, or non-action. By releasing the need to accumulate, we align ourselves more easily with the natural flow of the Tao, finding effortless effectiveness and peace.

Being without Ji Ji also involves a shift in how we view wealth and security. Instead of seeking safety and fulfillment through accumulation, it encourages us to find these qualities through alignment with the Tao and trust in the natural abundance of the universe.

It's important to note that this principle doesn't advocate for poverty or neglect of practical needs. Rather, it's about finding the right balance – having what we need without being burdened by excess. It's about recognizing that true wealth lies not in what we possess, but in our capacity to appreciate and flow with life.

Modern Application:

1. Minimalism: Embracing a lifestyle that focuses on essentials and experiences rather than accumulation of possessions.

2. Financial Wellbeing: Developing a healthier relationship with money, focusing on sufficiency and flow rather than hoarding.

3. Knowledge Management: Valuing the application and integration of knowledge rather than mere accumulation of information.

4. Time Management: Letting go of the need to "accumulate" achievements, focusing instead on meaningful experiences and growth.

5. Relationships: Cultivating quality connections rather than a large quantity of superficial relationships.

6. Environmental Sustainability: Reducing consumption and waste by resisting the urge to accumulate unnecessary goods.

7. Mental Health: Alleviating anxiety related to never having or being "enough" by cultivating contentment and trust.

8. Spiritual Practice: Focusing on deepening understanding and experience rather than accumulating spiritual knowledge or merits.

Practical steps:

- Regularly decluttering physical spaces and digital life
- Practicing mindfulness to become aware of the impulse to acquire or hoard
- Before making purchases, pausing to reflect on whether the item is truly needed
- Implementing a "one in, one out" rule for new acquisitions
- Engaging in practices of giving or sharing to counteract the tendency to accumulate
- Cultivating gratitude for what you already have
- Exploring experiences rather than acquiring things as a source of fulfillment
- Regularly assessing your possessions, information, and commitments to release what's no longer serving you

Reflection Questions:

1. In what areas of your life do you tend to accumulate excessively? How does this affect your wellbeing?

2. Can you recall a time when letting go of something led to a sense of freedom or new opportunities? What did this teach you?

3. How might your life change if you consistently practiced being without Ji Ji?

4. What fears or beliefs might be driving your need to accumulate in certain areas?

5. How does the idea of wealth through non-accumulation challenge or support your current views on success and security?

6. In what ways could embracing this principle enhance your relationships or sense of purpose?

7. How might practicing being without Ji Ji change your approach to personal growth or achievement?

Remember, being without Ji Ji is not about depriving yourself or rejecting the material world. It's about finding freedom, peace, and fulfillment through non-attachment and trust in the abundant flow of the Tao. As you explore this concept, pay attention to moments when letting go brings a sense of lightness, clarity, or unexpected gain. These can be glimpses of what it means to truly embody being without Ji Ji, aligning with the free-flowing, ever-abundant nature of the Tao.

Afterword

Dear Reader,

As we come to the close of this journey through the 81 aspects of Taoist wisdom, I hope you've found insights that resonate deeply with your own experience of life. The path of the Tao is not a destination to be reached, but a way of being to be lived. Each concept we've explored is a doorway to deeper understanding and alignment with the natural flow of existence.

Remember that the true essence of the Tao cannot be captured in words. These chapters are meant to serve as guideposts, inviting you to look beyond the words to your own direct experience. The real wisdom lies not in the pages of this book, but in how you embody these principles in your daily life.

As you move forward from here, I encourage you to continue your exploration of the Tao. Return to these chapters as needed, allowing different aspects to speak to you as your life unfolds. Practice the reflections and exercises regularly, and most importantly, remain open to the Tao as it manifests in every moment of your life.

The journey of awakening the sage within is ongoing. There will be times of clarity and times of confusion, moments of flow and moments of resistance. Embrace it all as part of the dance of yin and yang, knowing that each experience offers an opportunity for deeper alignment with the Tao.

May your path be filled with wisdom, peace, and the joy of living in harmony with the eternal Tao.

In oneness,

Azariah Samuel A.

Glossary of Key Taoist Terms:

Dao (Tao) - The Way; the fundamental nature of the universe

De (Te) - Virtue; the power that comes from alignment with the Tao

Wu Wei - Non-action; effortless action in alignment with the Tao

Yin and Yang - Complementary opposites that make up all aspects of life

Qi (Chi) - Life force or vital energy

Ziran - Naturalness; spontaneity

Pu - Simplicity; the uncarved block

Wu Xin - No-mind; a state of open awareness

Jing - Stillness; tranquility

Bibliography

Lao Tzu. Tao Te Ching. Translated by Stephen Mitchell. New York: Harper Perennial, 1992.

Watts, Alan. Tao: The Watercourse Way. New York: Pantheon, 1975.

Deng, Ming-Dao. 365 Tao: Daily Meditations. New York: HarperOne, 1992.

Cleary, Thomas. The Essential Tao. New York: HarperOne, 1993.